NCERT Practice

WorkBook

Mathematics
Math-Magic

❋arihant

Arihant Prakashan (School Division Series)

✴ arihant

Arihant Prakashan (School Division Series)

All Rights Reserved

卐 **Administrative & Production Offices**

Regd. Office
'Ramchhaya' 4577/15, Agarwal Road, Darya Ganj, New Delhi -110002
Tele: 011- 47630600, 43518550

卐 **Head Office**
Kalindi, TP Nagar, Meerut (UP) - 250002
Tel: 0121-7156203, 7156204

卐 **Sales & Support Offices**
Agra, Ahmedabad, Bengaluru, Bareilly, Chennai, Delhi, Guwahati, Hyderabad, Jaipur, Jhansi, Kolkata, Lucknow, Nagpur & Pune.

PO No : TXT-XX-XXXXXXX-X-XX

Published by Arihant Publications (India) Ltd.

For further information about the books published by Arihant, log on to www.arihantbooks.com or e-mail at info@arihantbooks.com

Follow us on    

PRODUCTION TEAM

Publishing Managers
Keshav Mohan, Amit Verma

Project Coordinator
Ashwani

Project Editor
Amit Tanwar

Cover Designer
Bilal Hashmi

Inner Designer
Ankit Saini

Proof Readers
Akash Sharma

Workbook, Why?

"Knowledge will not be with you for Long Unless You Practice"

This quotation answer the above question 'Workbook, Why?' perfectly, i.e. Workbooks are made to give the students practice required to achieve perfection & mastery in the subject. These are the only Workbooks, which are strictly based on NCERT, the only recommended books by Govt. of India & CBSE (reference Circular No. Acad-41/2015 dated 20th July 2015).

Given below is the detailed description of Workbook and some of its special features

ONLY WORKBOOK BASED ON NCERT

NCERT textbooks are the only textbooks, which have been prepared according to National Curriculum Framework, which discourages the idea of rote learning rather they focus on understanding and try to make the students able to identify the way of problem solving.

Keeping the importance of NCERT textbooks in mind we have prepared this Workbook, strictly based on NCERT content, this Workbook will complement NCERT by providing practice on the material given in each chapter of NCERT textbook, making the students understand the chapter completely.

WORKBOOK- PURPOSE, USE & FEATURES

This Workbook, through its numerous exercises having different variety of questions covering each and every fact of NCERT, will prove to be equally useful for both, Classroom and at Home. One more purpose of this Workbook is to provide the students a systematic practice of the content taught in the class and what they study in the textbooks.

Some special features of this workbook are

- Complete Coverage of each chapter for complete practice

- Different variety of questions; Fill in the Blanks, True-False, Matching, Multiple Choice Questions, Word Problems, etc.

- Many Questions given in each chapter are related with day-to-day activities making them interesting to solve.

- Keeps the students actively engaged with the content and develop enquiry skills.

WORKBOOK-DESIGNED TO IMPROVE SUBJECT ABILITIES

All the material given in this workbook is tailored to suit subject content with equal support on learning, which will surely help students to boost their abilities and confidence in the subject.

We look forward for the feedback from students, teachers and parents for the further improvement of the contents of this book. We will try to update the contents according to your feedback in further editions of this Workbook.

The Publisher

Contents

Chapter 1

Shapes and Space

1 Tick (✓) the objects which are inside and cross (✗) the objects which are outside.

2 Colour the picture which is bigger.

(i)

(ii)

(iii)

(iv)

3 Look at the pictures below. Tick (✓) the pictures which are biggest and cross (✗) the pictures which are smallest in each part.

(i)

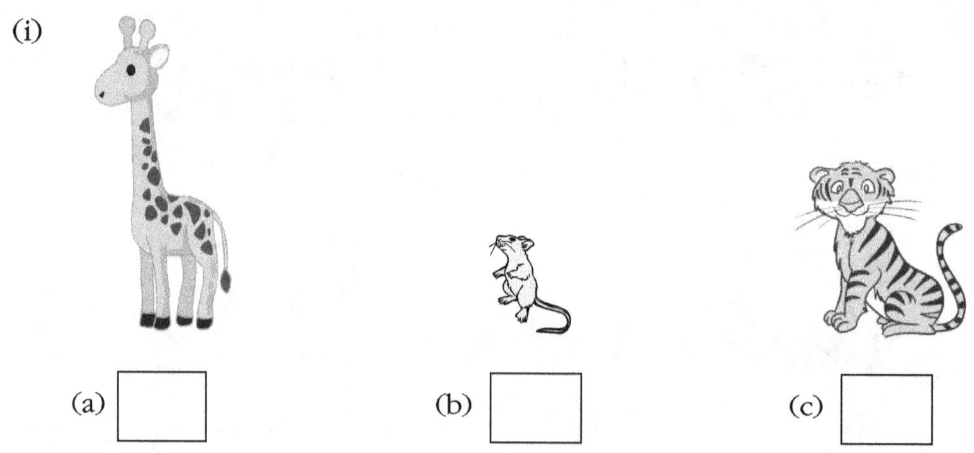

(a)   (b)   (c)

(ii)

(a)    (b)    (c)

(iii)

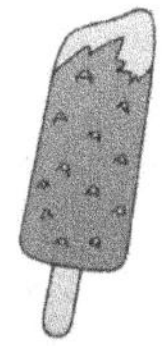

(a) 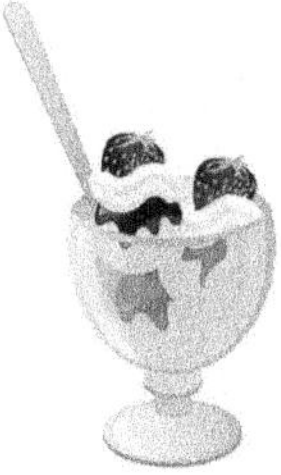   (b)    (c)

(iv)

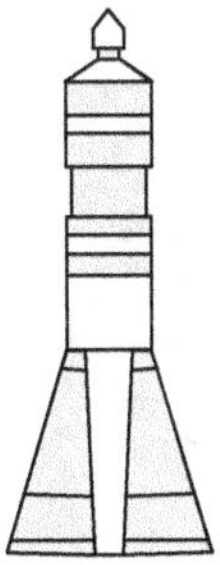

(a) 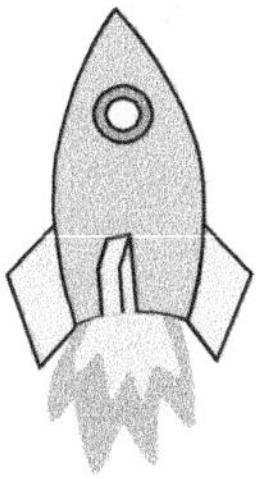   (b) 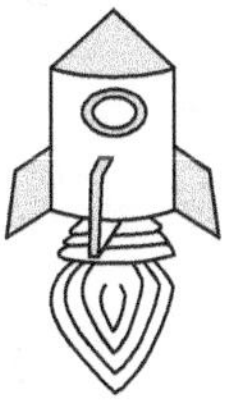   (c)

4 (i) Tick (✓) the pot at the bottom.

(ii) Tick (✓) book on the top.

(iii) Tick (✓) flower on the top.

(iv) Tick (✓) rabbit at the bottom.

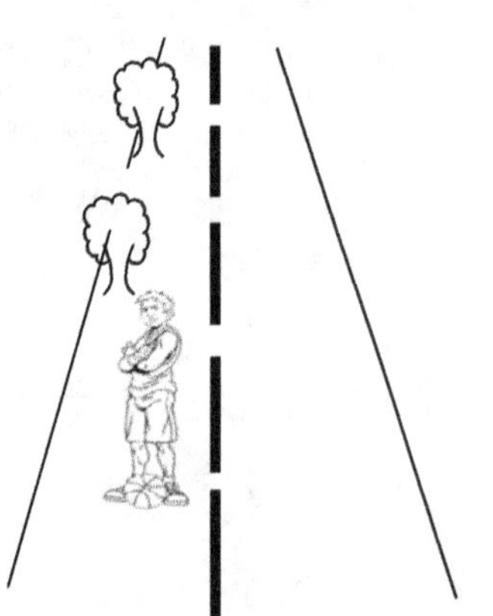

5 (i) Tick (✓) the tree which is nearer to the boy.

(ii) Tick (✓) the person who is farther from the bus.

(iii) Tick (✓) the car which is nearer to the traffic signal.

6 (i) Tick (✓) the cat which is nearest to the rat.

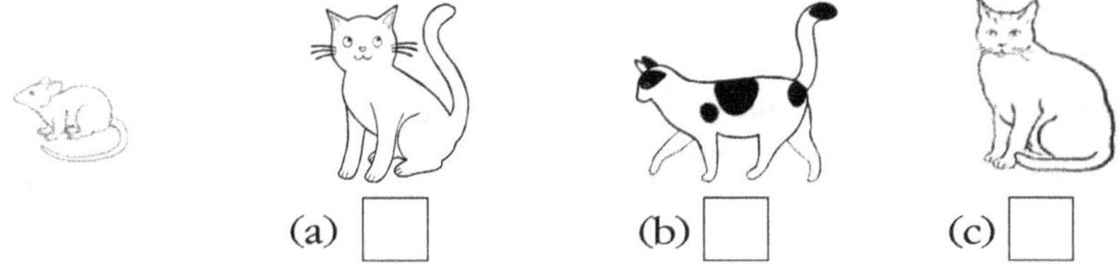

(a) ☐   (b) ☐   (c) ☐

(ii) Tick (✓) the car which is farthest from the boy.

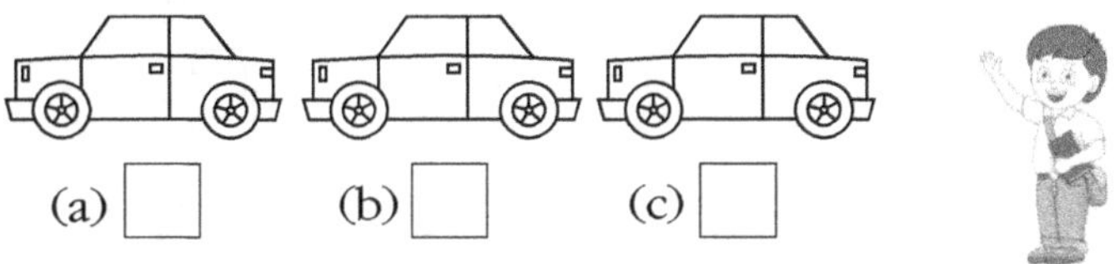

(a) ☐   (b) ☐   (c) ☐

(iii) Tick (✔) the child which is nearest to the bus.

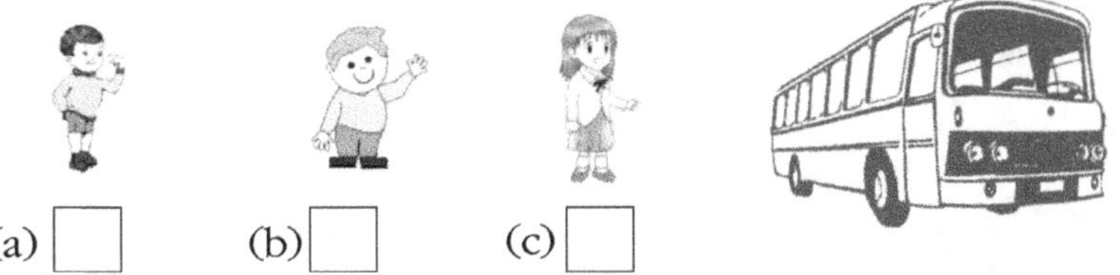

(a) ☐   (b) ☐   (c) ☐

(iv) Tick (✔) the bird which is farthest from the tree.

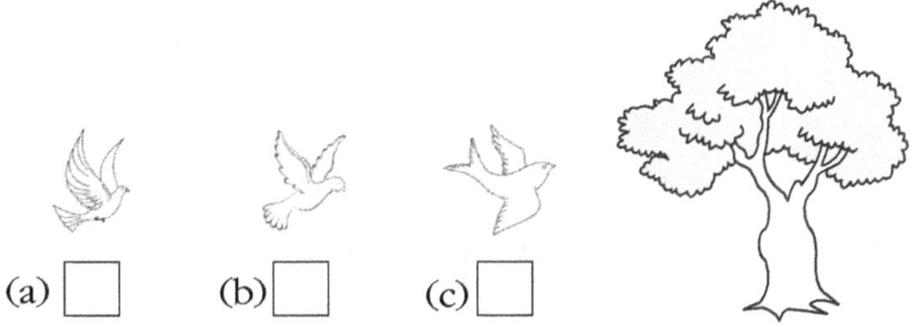

(a) ☐   (b) ☐   (c) ☐

7 **Fill in the blanks.**

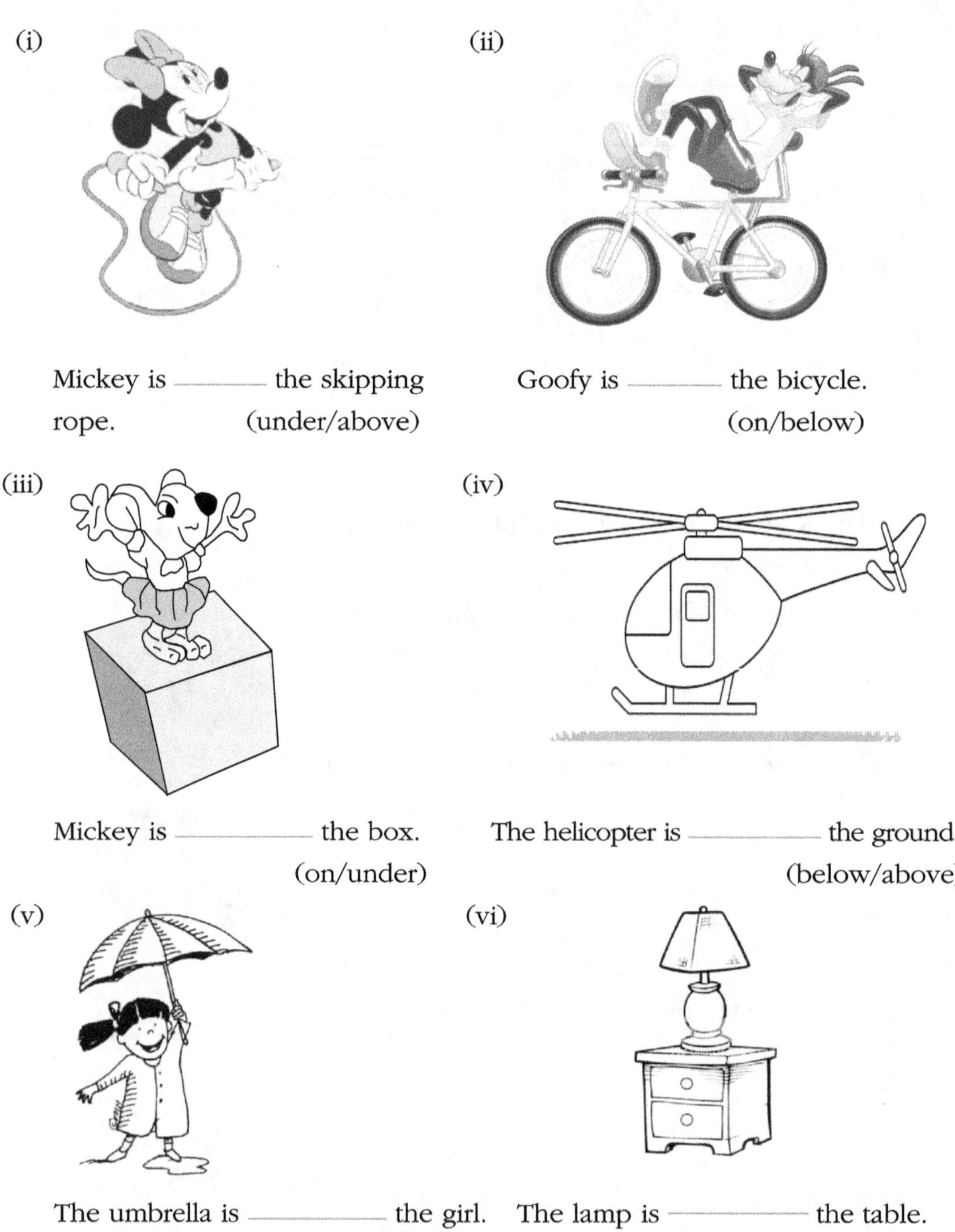

(i) Mickey is ———— the skipping rope. (under/above)

(ii) Goofy is ———— the bicycle. (on/below)

(iii) Mickey is ———— the box. (on/under)

(iv) The helicopter is ———— the ground. (below/above)

(v) The umbrella is ———— the girl. (below/above)

(vi) The lamp is ———— the table. (on/under)

8 Tick (✔) on ◯ (Circle) shapes and cross (✘) on ▭ (Rectangle) shapes.

(i)

(a) 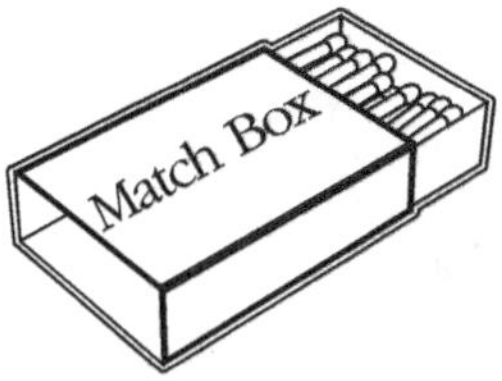 (b)  (c)

(ii)

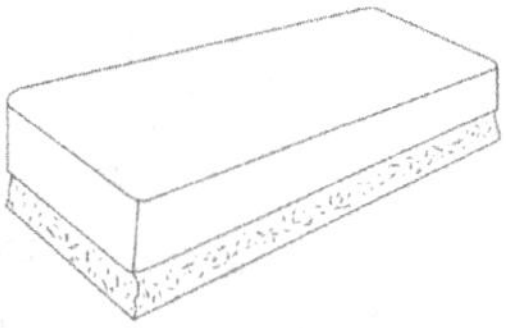

(a) 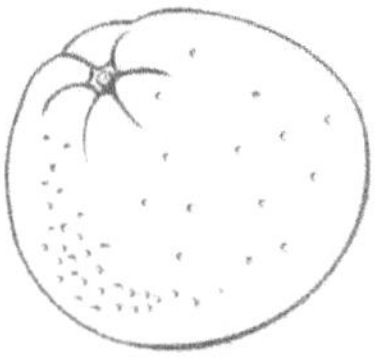 (b) 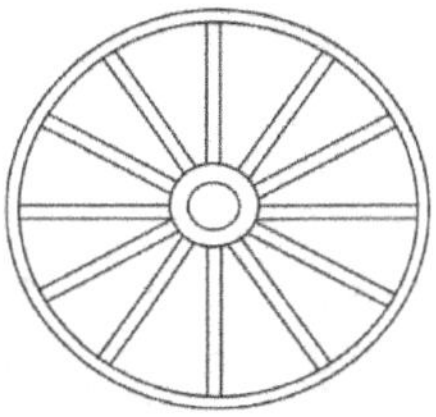 (c)

(iii)

(a) 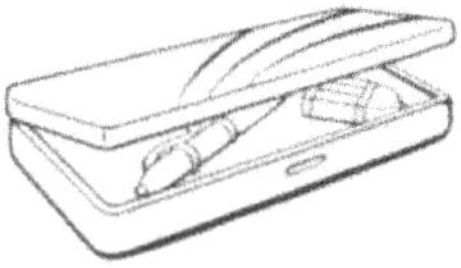 (b)  (c)

(iv)

(a) 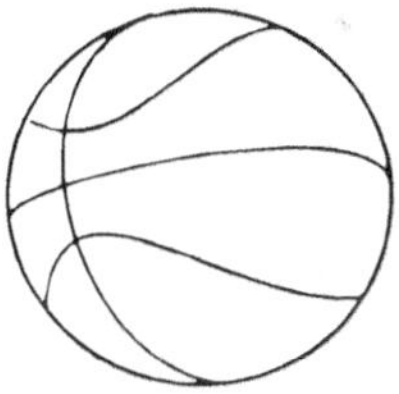 (b)  (c)

9 Given below are some figures numbered from (i) to (ix), colour these figures according to the instructions given below.

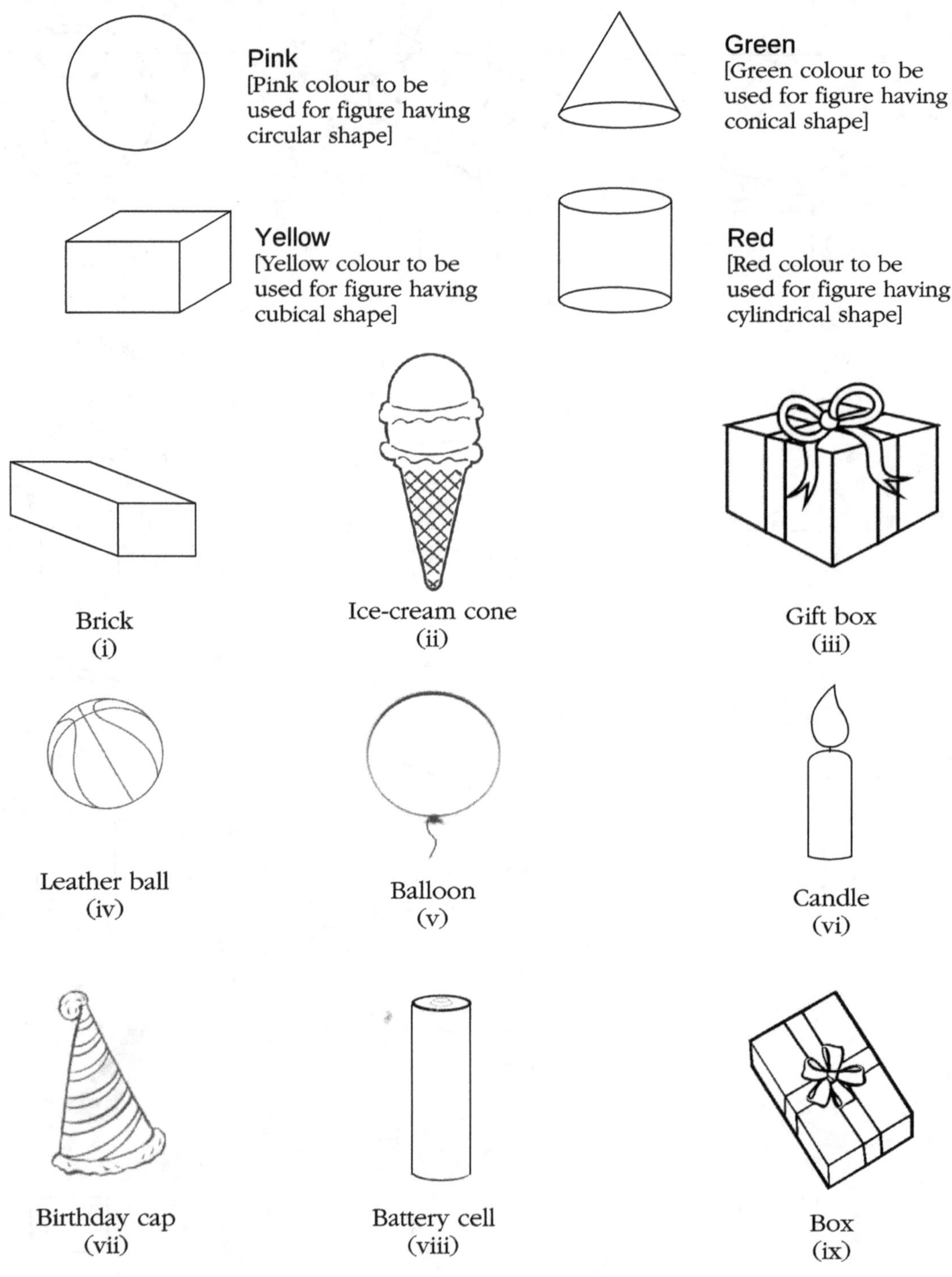

Brick
(i)

Ice-cream cone
(ii)

Gift box
(iii)

Leather ball
(iv)

Balloon
(v)

Candle
(vi)

Birthday cap
(vii)

Battery cell
(viii)

Box
(ix)

Column I	Column II
(i)	(a) Match box
(ii)	(b)
(iii) Shoe box	(c) Chalk box
(iv)	(d)
(v)	(e)

11 (i) Tick (✓) the object which can slide.

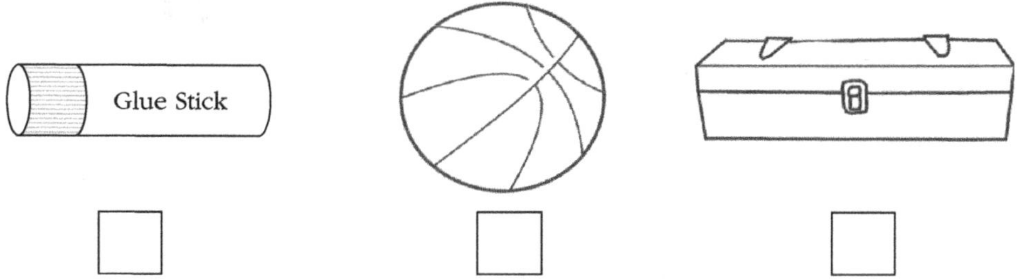

(ii) Tick (✔) the object which can roll.

(a) 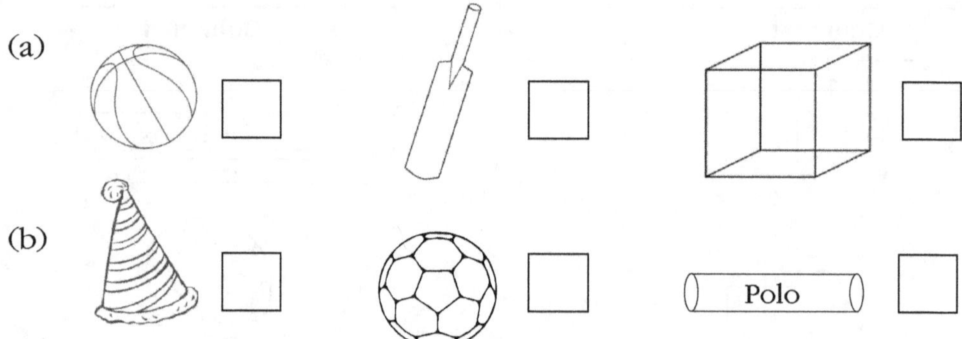

(b) 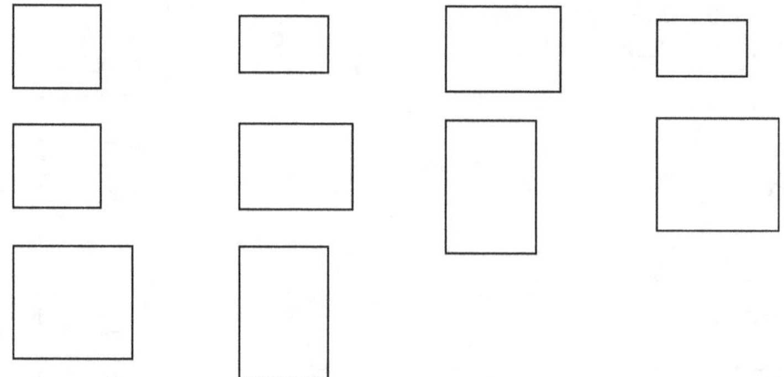

12 Colour the shapes of same size with same colour.

13 Match the similar shapes. One has been done for you.

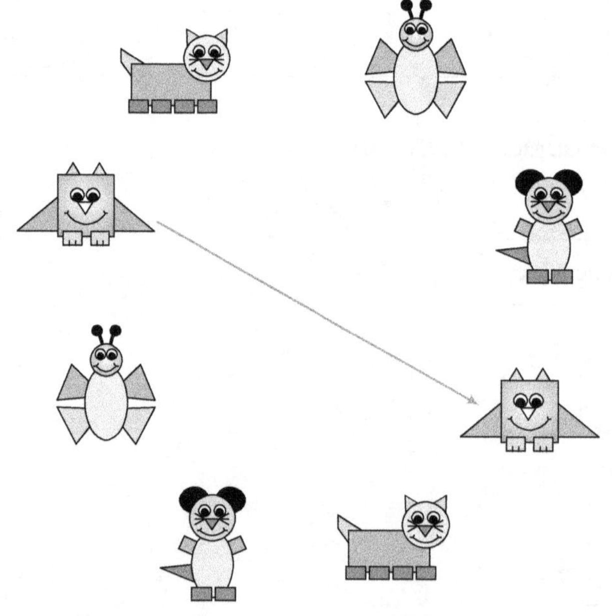

14 Colour the figures with the help of instructions given in each part.

(i) △ = Red,   ☐ = Blue,   ◯ = Yellow,   ▭ = Green

(ii) ☐ = Blue,   △ = Green,   ▭ = Red,

◯ = Orange,

Numbers from One to Nine

1 Draw the lines to show that each group has equal number of objects. One has been done for you.

(i)

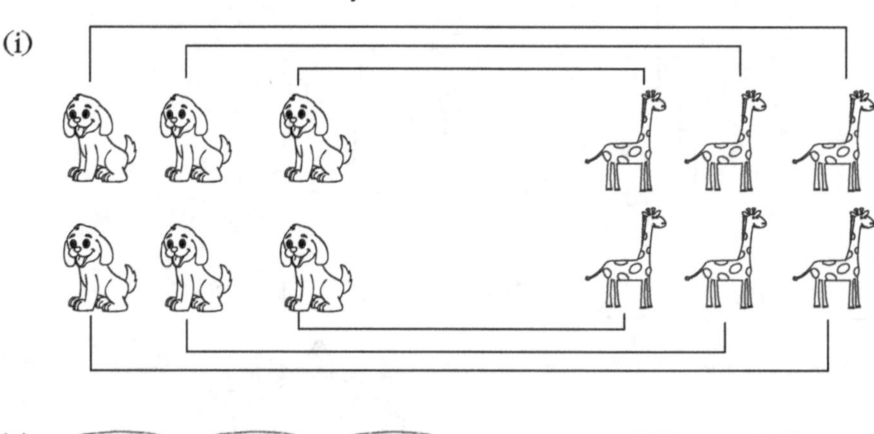

(ii)

(iii)

(iv)

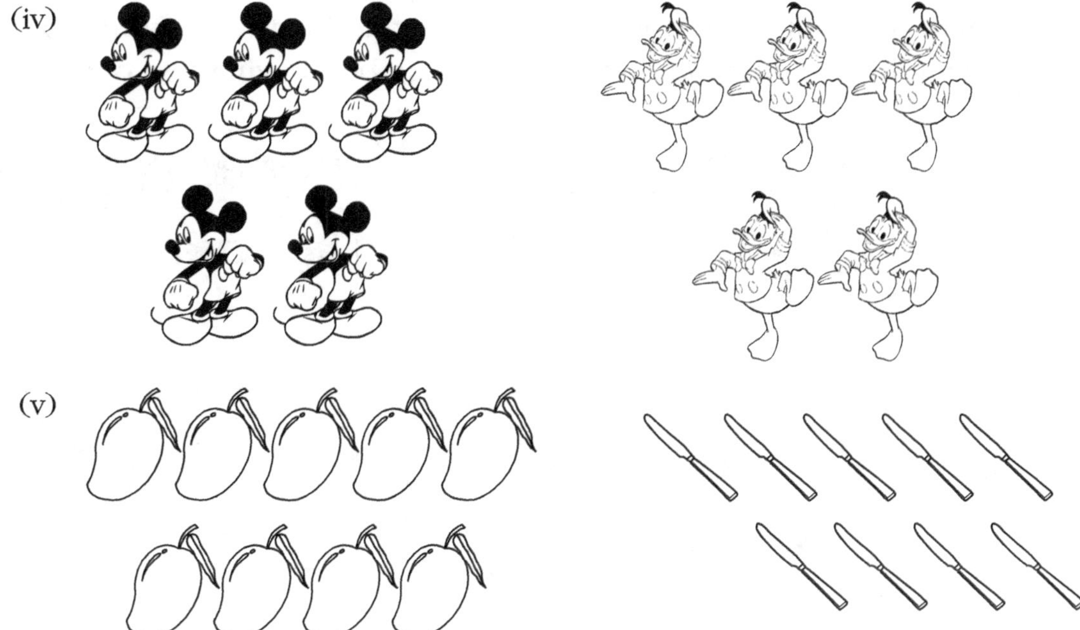

(v)

2 Count and write the number of birds alongwith the number name.

	Number	Name
(i)		
(ii)		
(iii)		
(iv)		
(v)		
(vi)		
(vii)		
(viii)		

3 Count the number of objects in each box and mark (✓) on the box having more objects and mark (✗) on the box having less objects.

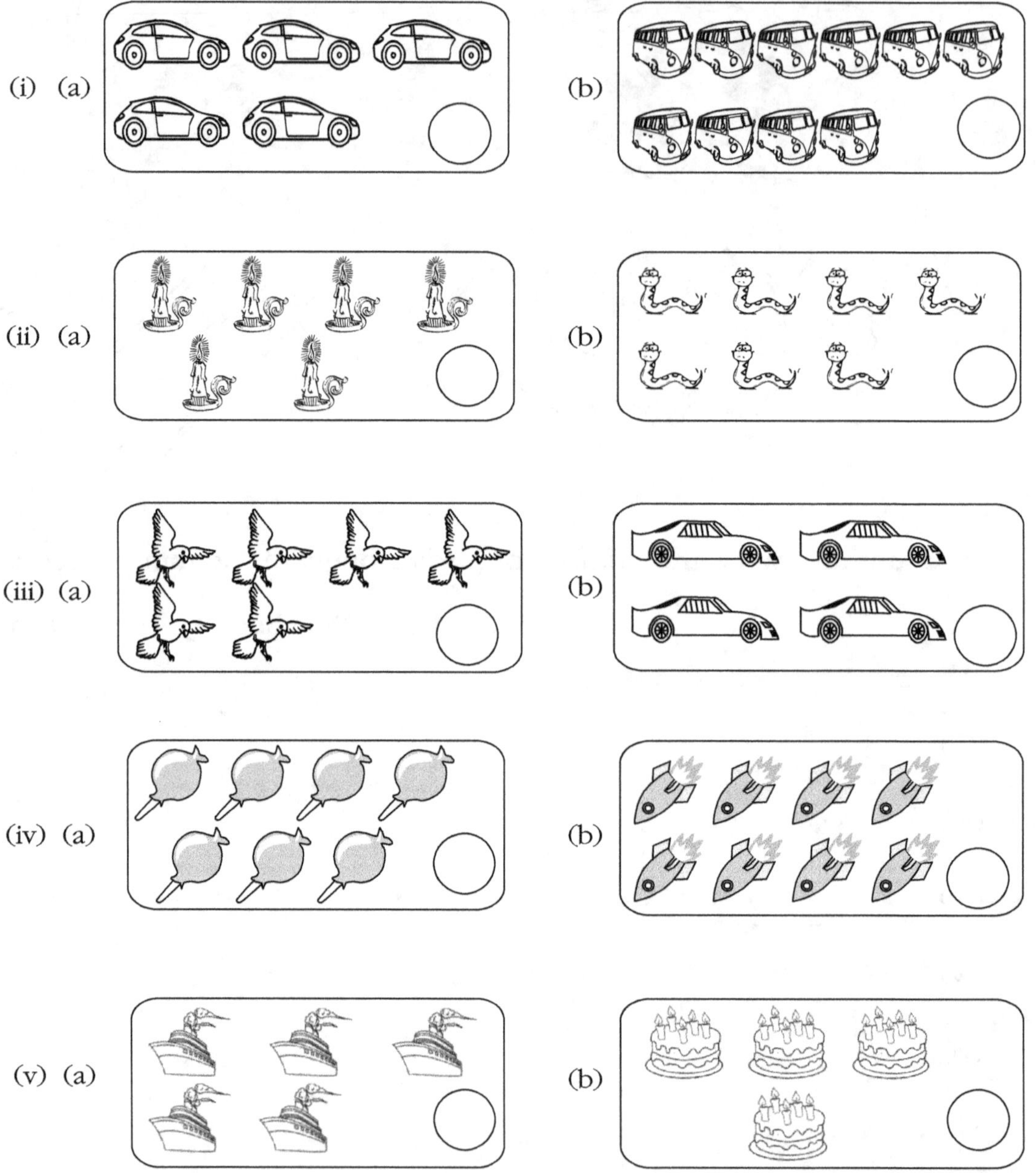

(i) (a)   (b)

(ii) (a)   (b)

(iii) (a)   (b)

(iv) (a)   (b)

(v) (a)   (b)

4 Count the number of circles given in column I and match them with the same number of objects given in column II.

Column I		Column II
(i) ◯◯◯◯◯	(a)	STOP STOP STOP
(ii) ◯◯◯◯◯◯	(b)	🧺🧺🧺🧺
(iii) ◯◯◯◯	(c)	✾✾✾✾✾
(iv) ◯◯◯◯◯◯◯	(d)	🔔🔔🔔🔔 🔔🔔
(v) ◯◯◯	(e)	☆☆☆☆☆ ☆☆

5 Join the dots in order to complete the figure and then colour it.

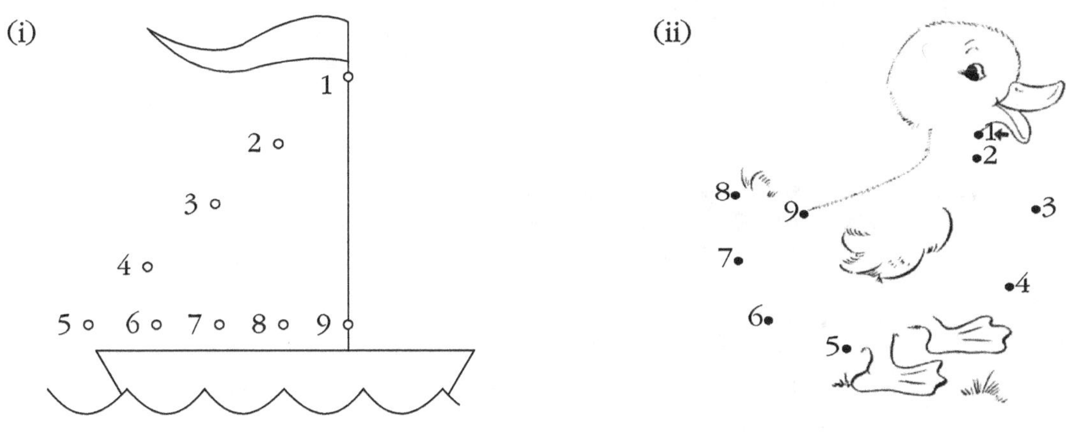

6 Count the number of objects given in column I and match them with the correct number given in column II.

Column I	Column II
(i)	 (a) 4
(ii)	 (b) 6
(iii)	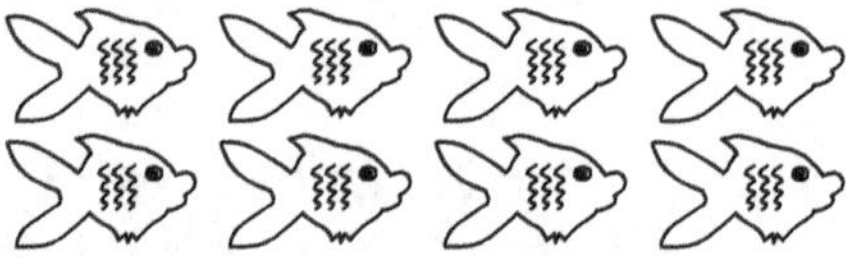 (c) 5
(iv)	 (d) 7
(v)	 (e) 9
(vi)	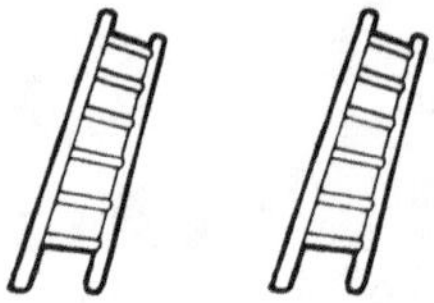 (f) 8
(vii)	 (g) 3
(viii)	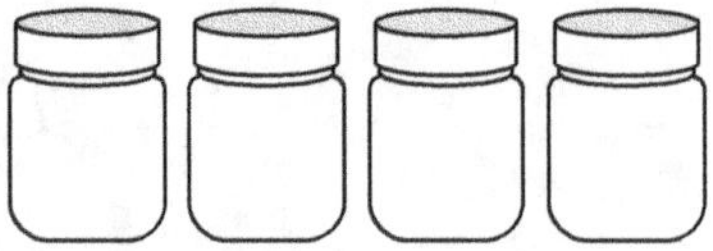 (h) 2

7 Make the group of objects according to the number given below each box. One has been done for you.

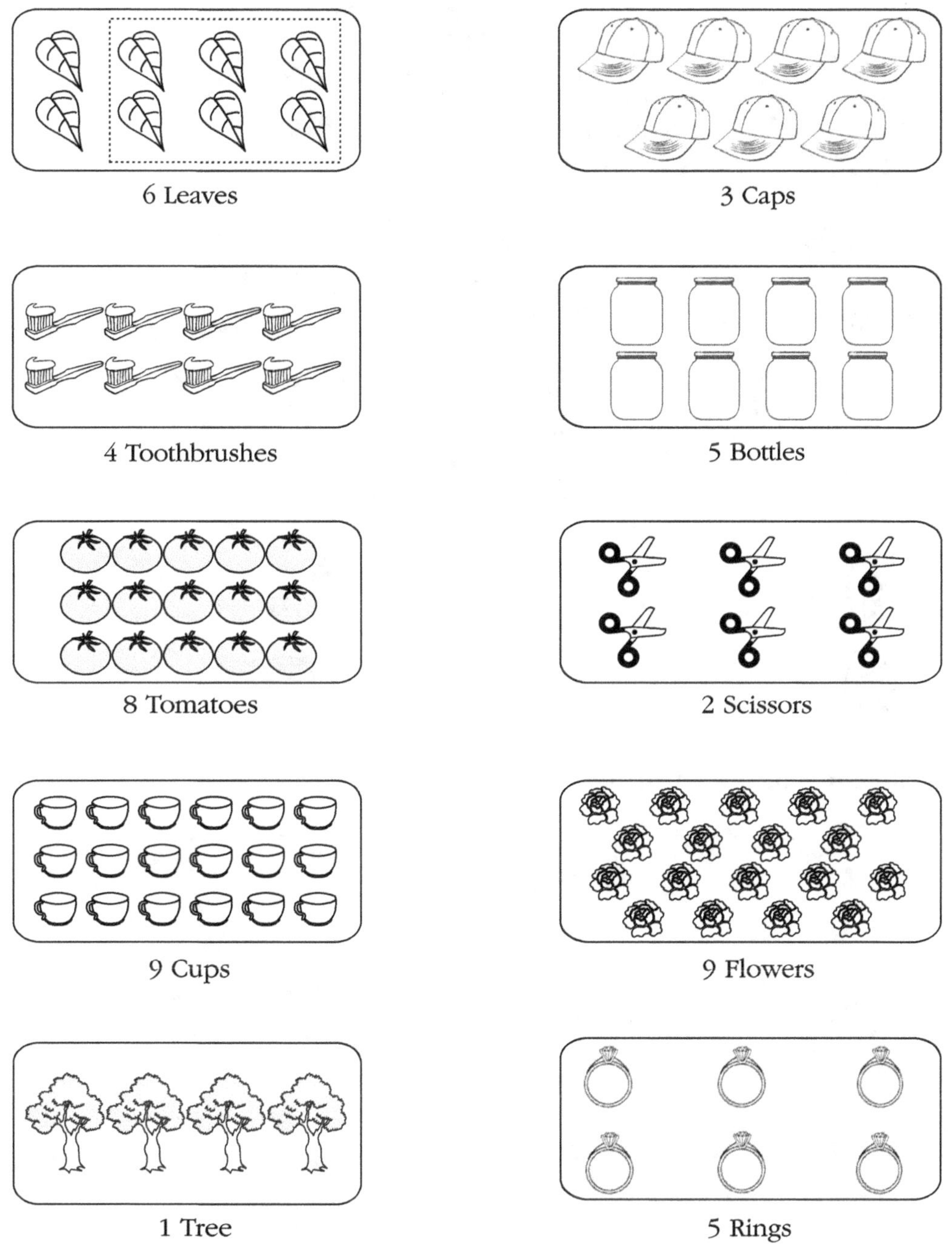

6 Leaves

3 Caps

4 Toothbrushes

5 Bottles

8 Tomatoes

2 Scissors

9 Cups

9 Flowers

1 Tree

5 Rings

8 Count and write the number of each animal.

(i) = _______________ (ii) = _______________

(iii) = _______________ (iv) = _______________

9 Write the missing number.

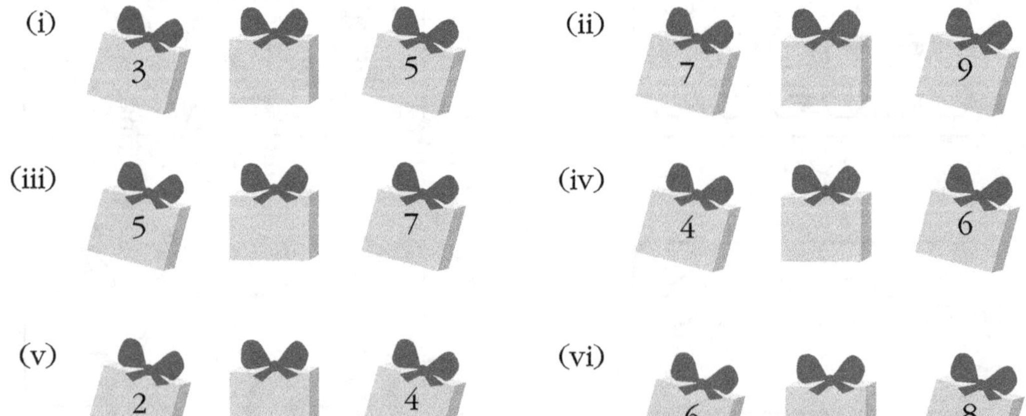

(i) 3 __ 5   (ii) 7 __ 9

(iii) 5 __ 7   (iv) 4 __ 6

(v) 2 __ 4   (vi) 6 __ 8

10 Write the numbers before and after the given numbers.

	Before			After
(i)		3	(ii)	8
(iii)		5	(iv)	2
(v)		8	(vi)	4
(vii)		9	(viii)	6
(ix)		7	(x)	1

11 Count and write the number of objects in each part.

(i)

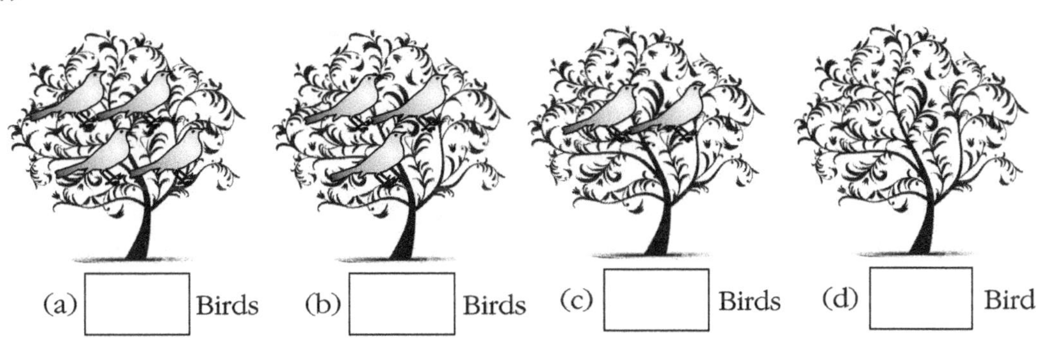

(a) ☐ Birds   (b) ☐ Birds   (c) ☐ Birds   (d) ☐ Bird

(ii)

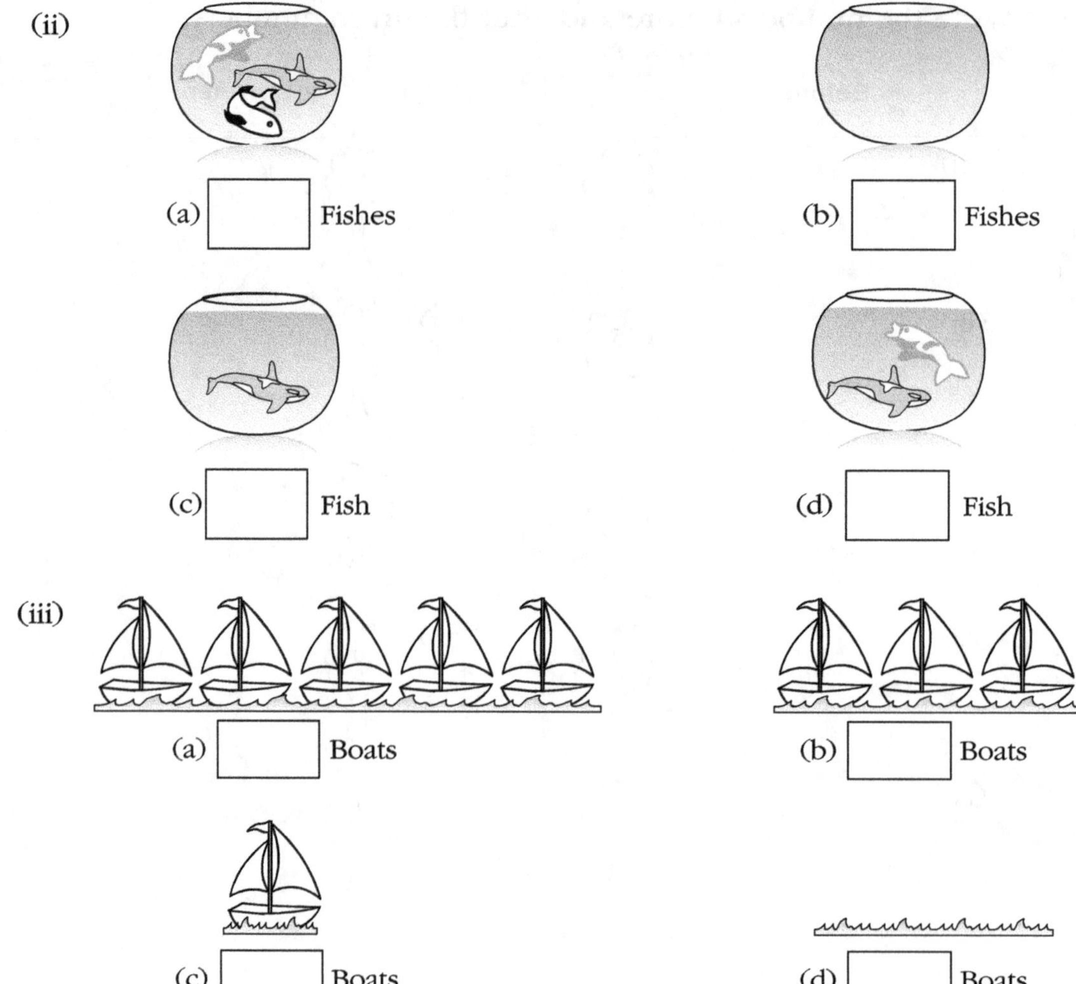

(a) ___ Fishes

(b) ___ Fishes

(c) ___ Fish

(d) ___ Fish

(iii)

(a) ___ Boats

(b) ___ Boats

(c) ___ Boats

(d) ___ Boats

Addition

1 Write the number which is one more than the number of objects given below. One has been done for you.

		One more	Number
(i)		+ =	4
(ii)		+ =	
(iii)		+ =	
(iv)		+ =	
(v)		+ =	

2 How many altogether? One has been done for you.

(i)

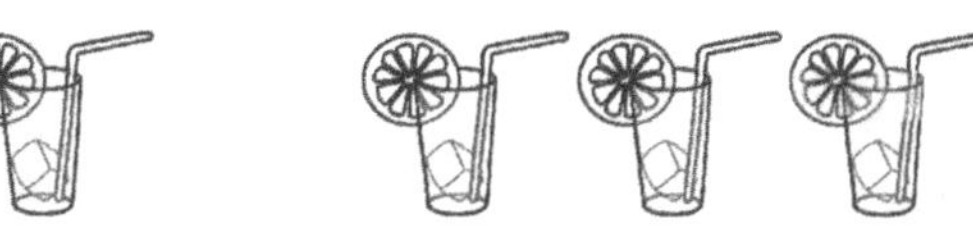

| 2 | drinks | and | 1 | drink | = | 3 | drinks. |

(ii) 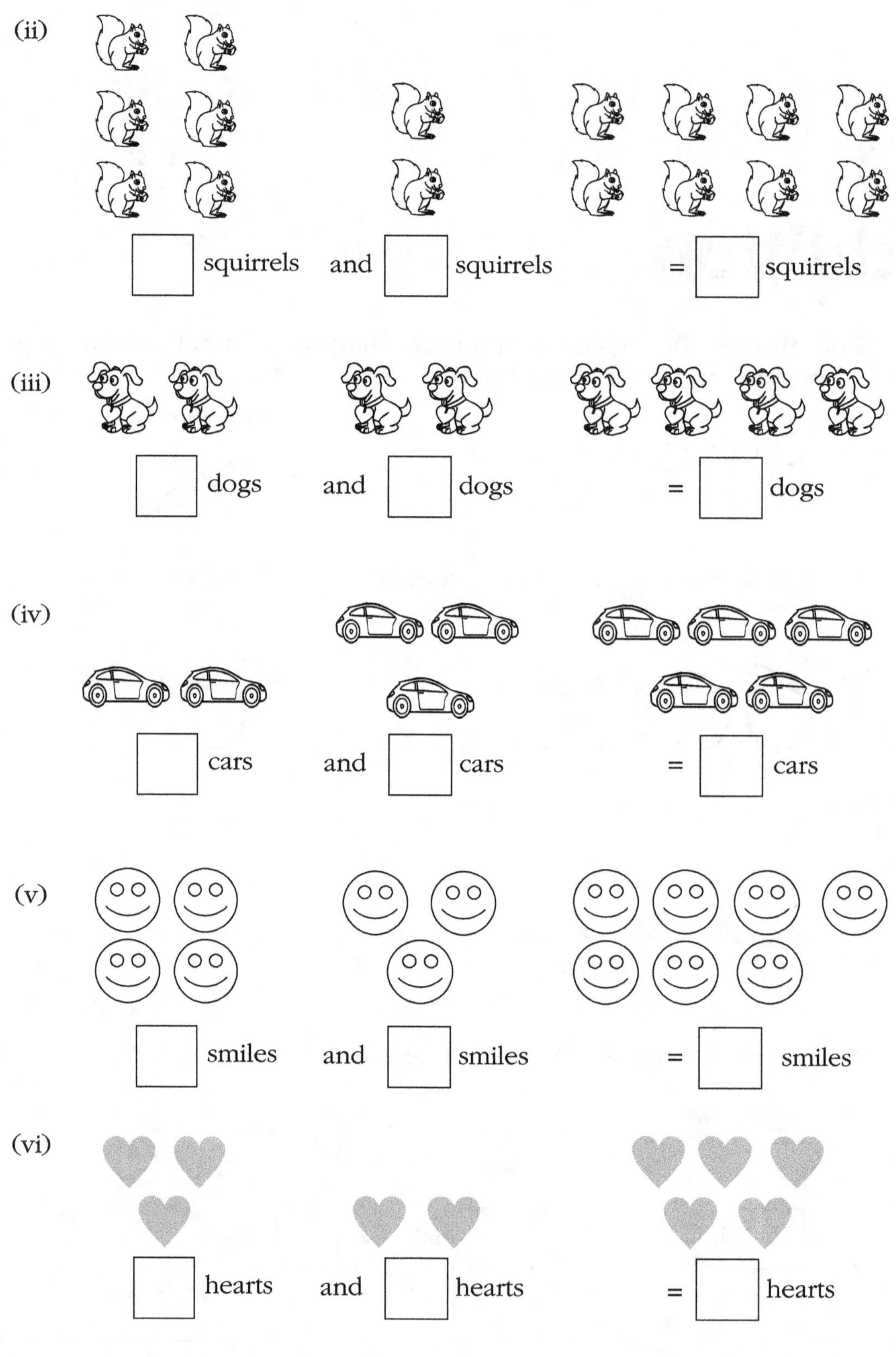

[ ] squirrels   and   [ ] squirrels   =   [ ] squirrels

(iii)

[ ] dogs   and   [ ] dogs   =   [ ] dogs

(iv)

[ ] cars   and   [ ] cars   =   [ ] cars

(v)

[ ] smiles   and   [ ] smiles   =   [ ] smiles

(vi)

[ ] hearts   and   [ ] hearts   =   [ ] hearts

3 Count the objects and write their number in the boxes given below.
Also, add them and write the result in the last box.

(i)

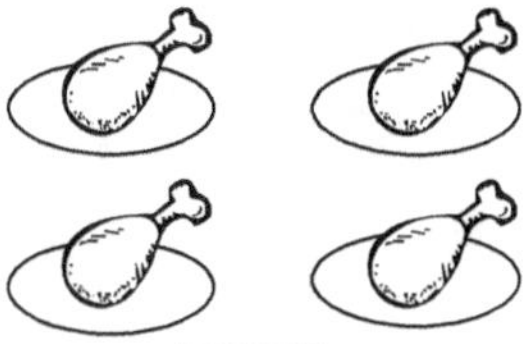

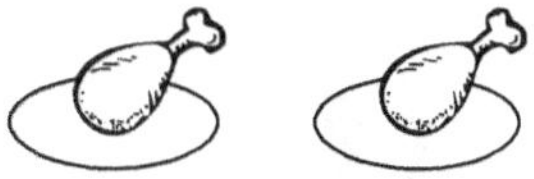

☐ + ☐ = ☐

(ii)

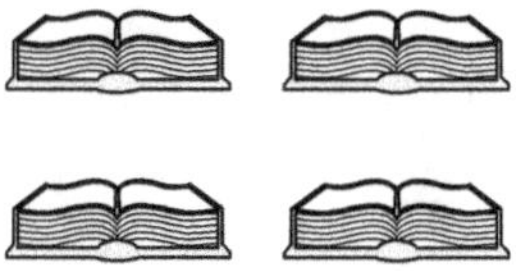

☐ + ☐ = ☐

(iii)

☐ + ☐ = ☐

(iv)

☐ + ☐ = ☐

(v)

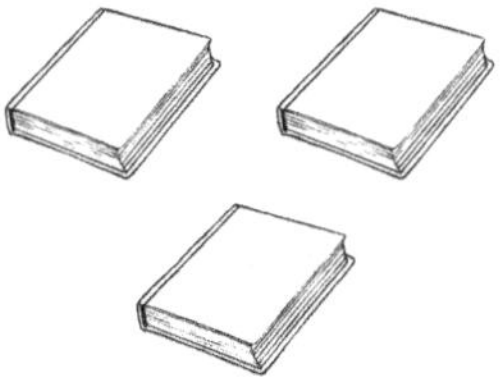

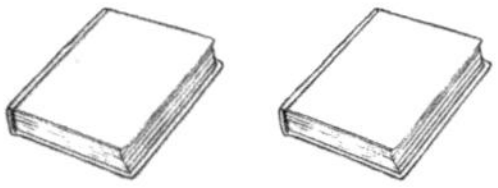

☐ + ☐ = ☐

(vi)

$\Box$ + $\Box$ = $\Box$

(vii)

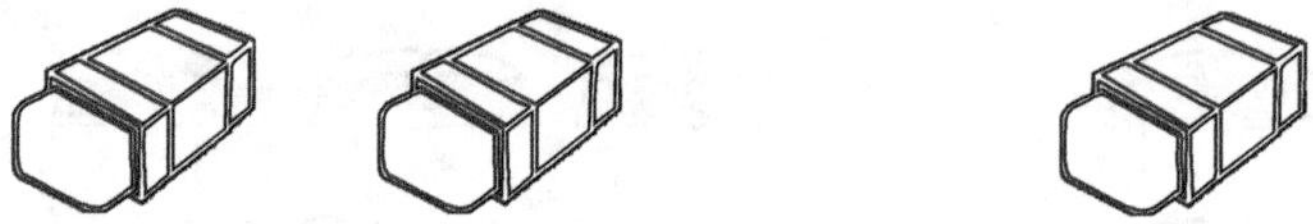

$\Box$ + $\Box$ = $\Box$

(viii)

$\Box$ + $\Box$ = $\Box$

4 **Match the following. One has been done for you.**

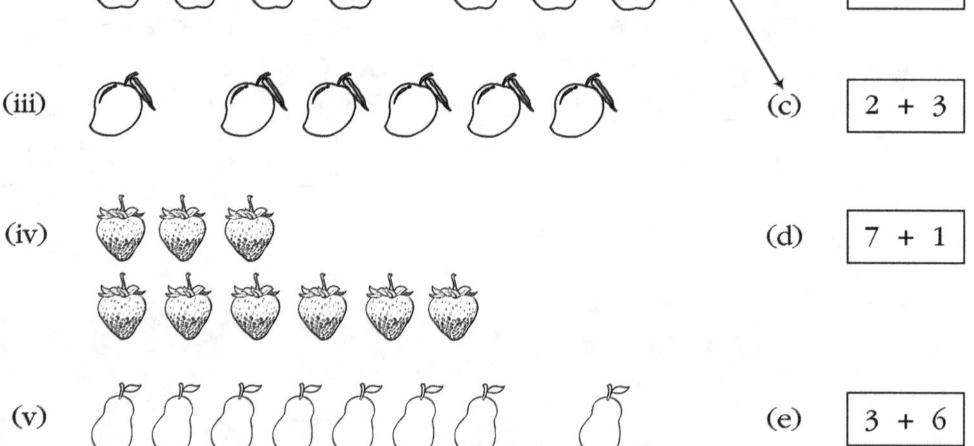

(i)   (a) $4 + 3$

(ii)   (b) $1 + 5$

(iii)   (c) $2 + 3$

(iv)   (d) $7 + 1$

(v)   (e) $3 + 6$

5 Add the given objects and circle the correct answer in the box. One has been done for you.

(i)   +   =   2,   3,   ④

(ii)   +   =   2,   3,   4

(iii)   +   =   4,   5,   6

(iv)   +   =   7,   8,   9

(v)   +   =   7,   8,   9

(vi)   +   =   4,   5,   6

6 Add and match. One has been done for you.

(i) $3 + 1$ I.   (a) $3 + 5$

(ii) $6 + 2$ II.   (b) $4 + 1$

(iii) $3 + 4$ III.   (c) $2 + 2$

(iv) $3 + 6$ IV.   (d) $1 + 8$

(v) $5 + 0$ V.   (e) $2 + 5$

(vi) $1 + 2$ VI.   (f) $2 + 1$

7 Add the numbers and fill the boxes.

(i) $4 + 3 = \Box$

(ii) $7 + 1 = \Box$

(iii) $2 + 4 = \Box$

(iv) $3 + 5 = \Box$

(v) $4 + 0 = \Box$

(vi) $3 + 6 = \Box$

(vii) $7 + 2 = \Box$

(viii) $1 + 8 = \Box$

(ix) $0 + 8 = \Box$

(x) $3 + 2 = \Box$

(xi) $5 + 4 = \Box$

(xii) $2 + 5 = \Box$

8 Write the missing numerals.

(i) $\Box + \Box = 7$

(ii) $\Box + \Box = 6$

(iii) $\Box + \Box = 3$

(iv) $\Box + \Box = 9$

(v) $\Box + \Box = 5$

(vi) $\Box + \Box = 4$

(vii) $\Box + \Box = 1$

(viii) $\Box + \Box = 8$

9 In each tree, circle any two leaves that have a sum shown on its stem. One has been done for you.

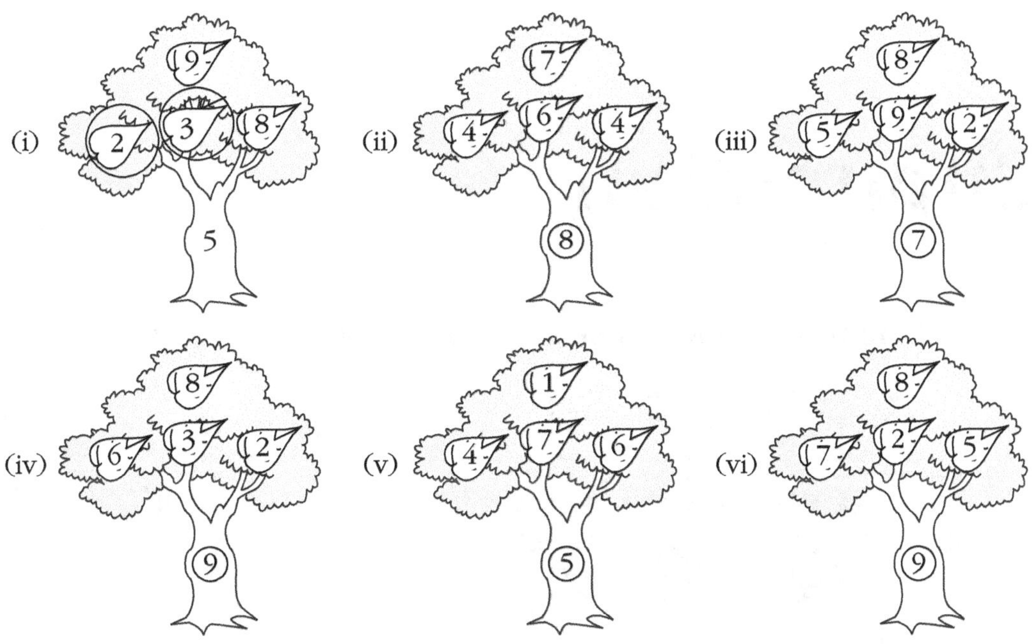

10 Problems based on addition.

(i) There are 5 frogs. 3 more frogs came. How many altogether?

(ii) Jack has 4 flowers. His friend gave him 3 more. How many flowers does he have now?

(iii) Tom had 7 pens. John had 1 pen. How many pens they both had?

Chapter 4

Subtraction

1 Fill the boxes. One has been done for you.

(i) 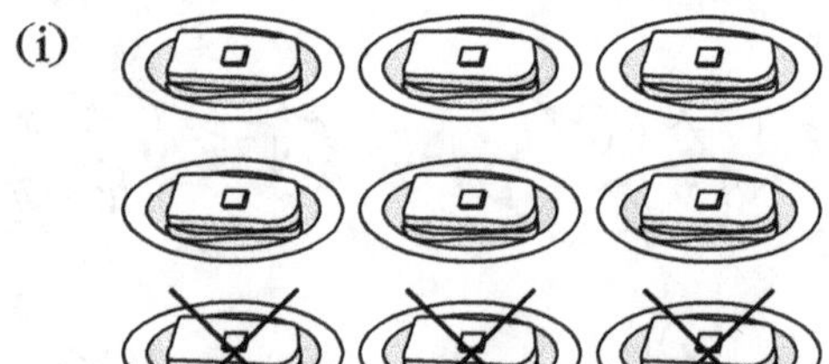

From | 9 | Take away | 3 | Left | 6

9 − 3 = 6

(ii)

From | | Take away | | Left |

☐ − ☐ = ☐

(iii) 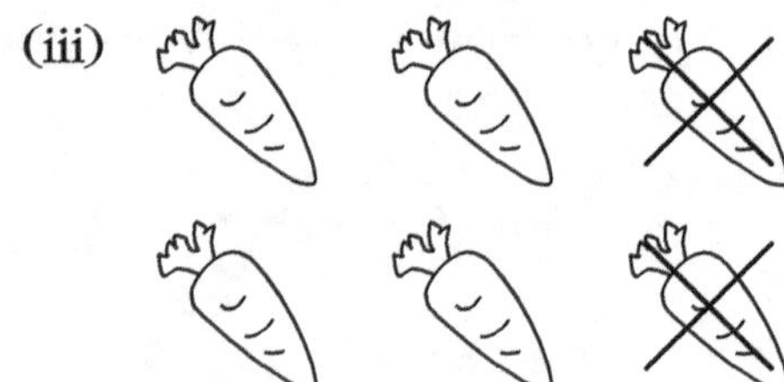

From | | Take away | | Left |

☐ − ☐ = ☐

(iv) 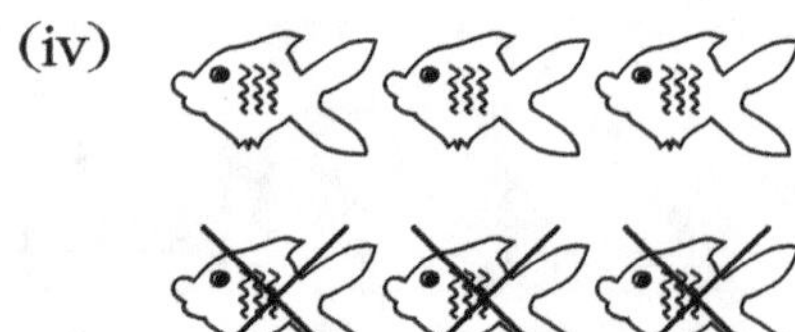

From | | Take away | | Left |

☐ − ☐ = ☐

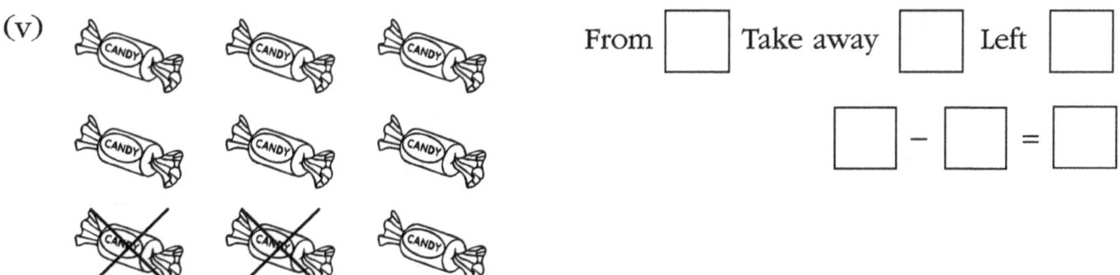

(v)

From ⬜ Take away ⬜ Left ⬜

⬜ – ⬜ = ⬜

2 Count and subtract. One has been done for you.

(i)

8 – 3 = 5

(ii)

⬜ – ⬜ = ⬜

(iii)

⬜ – ⬜ = ⬜

(iv)  – 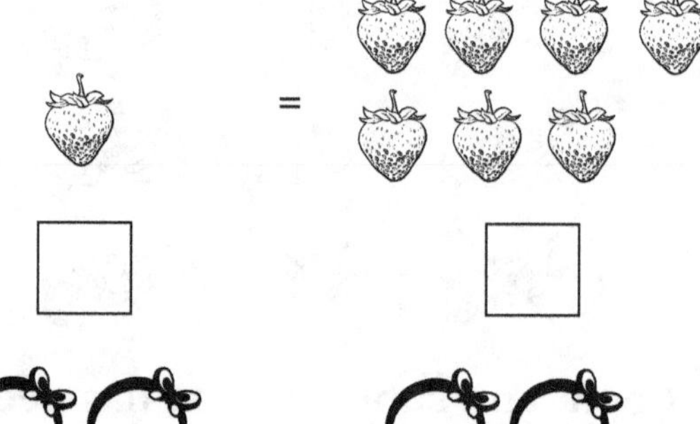 =

$$\Box \quad - \quad \Box \quad = \quad \Box$$

(v) 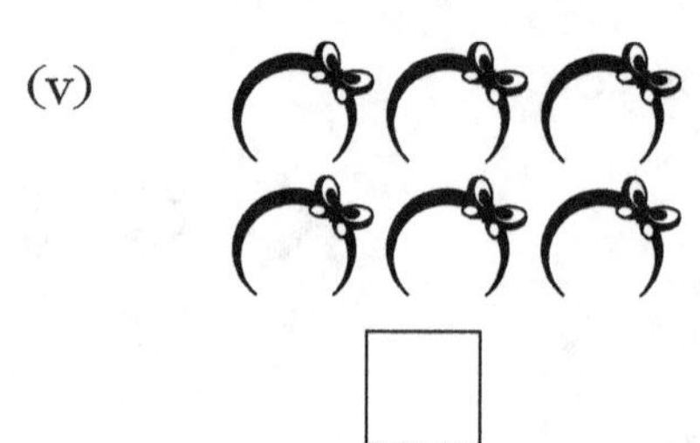 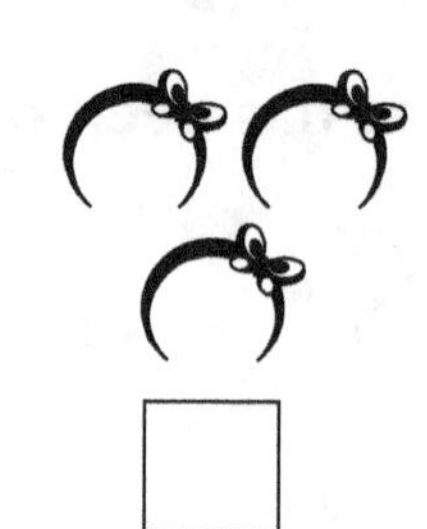 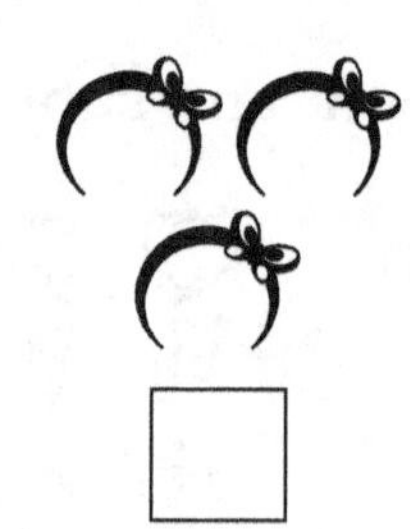

$$\Box \quad - \quad \Box \quad = \quad \Box$$

3 Subtract and match. One has been done for you.

(i) $8 - 2 =$

(ii) $9 - 9 =$

(iii) $6 - 5 =$

(iv) $6 - 4 =$

(v) $5 - 2 =$

| 0 |
| 1 |
| 2 |
| 3 |
| 4 |
| 5 |
| 6 |
| 7 |
| 8 |
| 9 |

(vi) $9 - 2 =$

(vii) $9 - 0 =$

(viii) $9 - 5 =$

(ix) $8 - 0 =$

(x) $6 - 1 =$

4 Solve the following.

(i) $\quad 9$
$\quad -4$
$\quad \overline{}$

(ii) $\quad 7$
$\quad -3$
$\quad \overline{}$

(iii) $\quad 9$
$\quad -7$
$\quad \overline{}$

(iv) $\quad 6$
$\quad -3$
$\quad \overline{}$

5 Write the missing numbers.

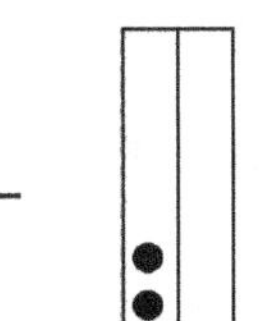

(i) 7 – 3 = ☐

(ii) ☐ – 6 = 3

(iii) 5 – ☐ = 1

(iv) ☐ – 3 = 5

(v) 9 – ☐ = 9

(vi) 3 – 0 = ☐

(vii) 7 – ☐ = 5

(viii) 5 – ☐ = 0

(ix) ☐ – 0 = 8

6 Subtract and fill in the domino. One has been done for you.

(i) 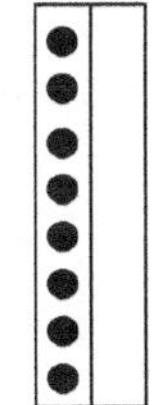 – =

(ii) – =

(iii) – =

(iv) – =

(v) 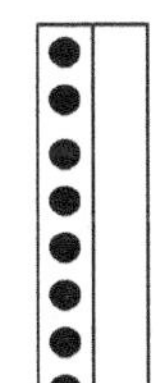 – =

7 **Problems based on subtraction.**

(i) Julie has 9 dolls. She gave 4 dolls to Anna. How many dolls does Julie have now?

(ii) James has 7 toy cars. 3 toy cars broke. How many toy cars are left with him?

(iii) John's mom buys 8 apples. John eats some of them. There are 3 left. How many apples did John eat?

(iv) Marry has 9 marbles. She lost 6 of them. How many marbles does she have now?

(v) Rohan bought 8 bats. Some of them broke. 5 bats are left now. How many bats broke?

Chapter 5

Numbers from Ten to Twenty

1 Make a group of objects as indicated in each part. One has been done for you.

(i)

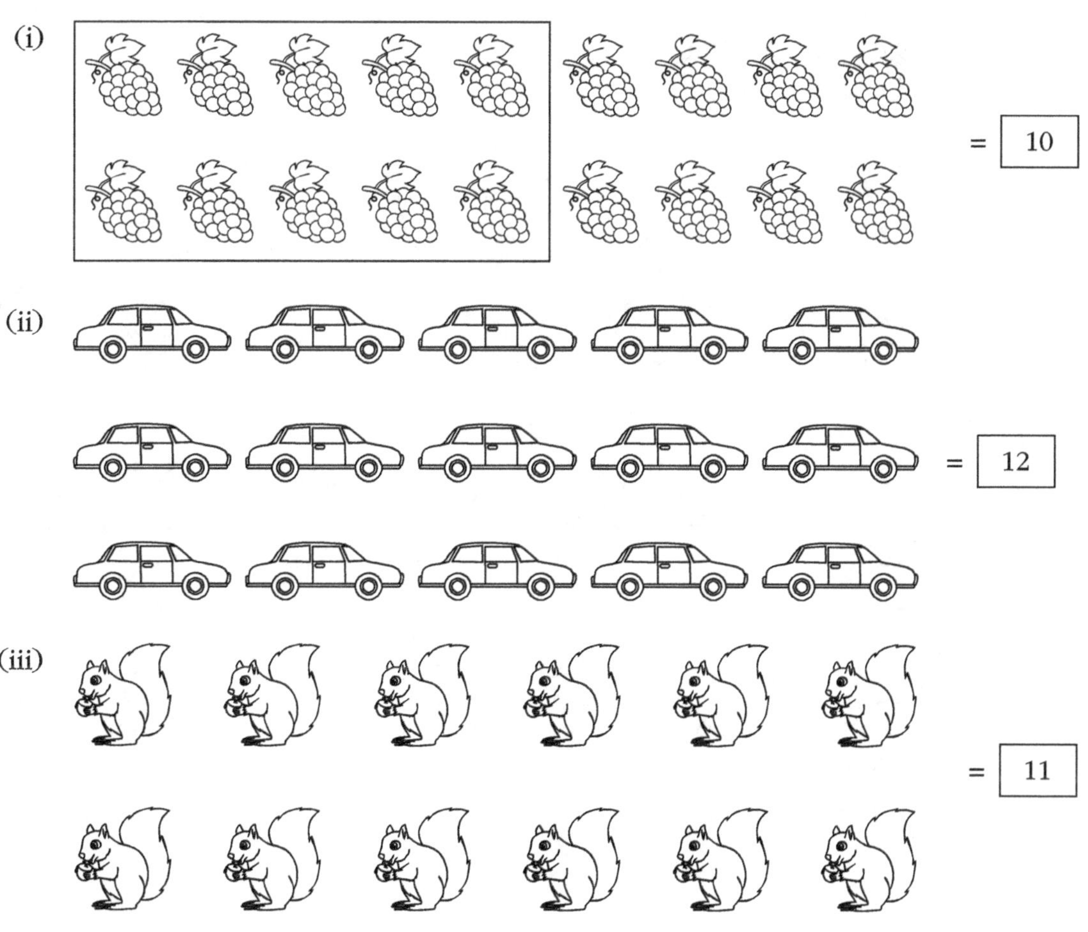

= [10]

(ii)

= [12]

(iii)

= [11]

(iv) 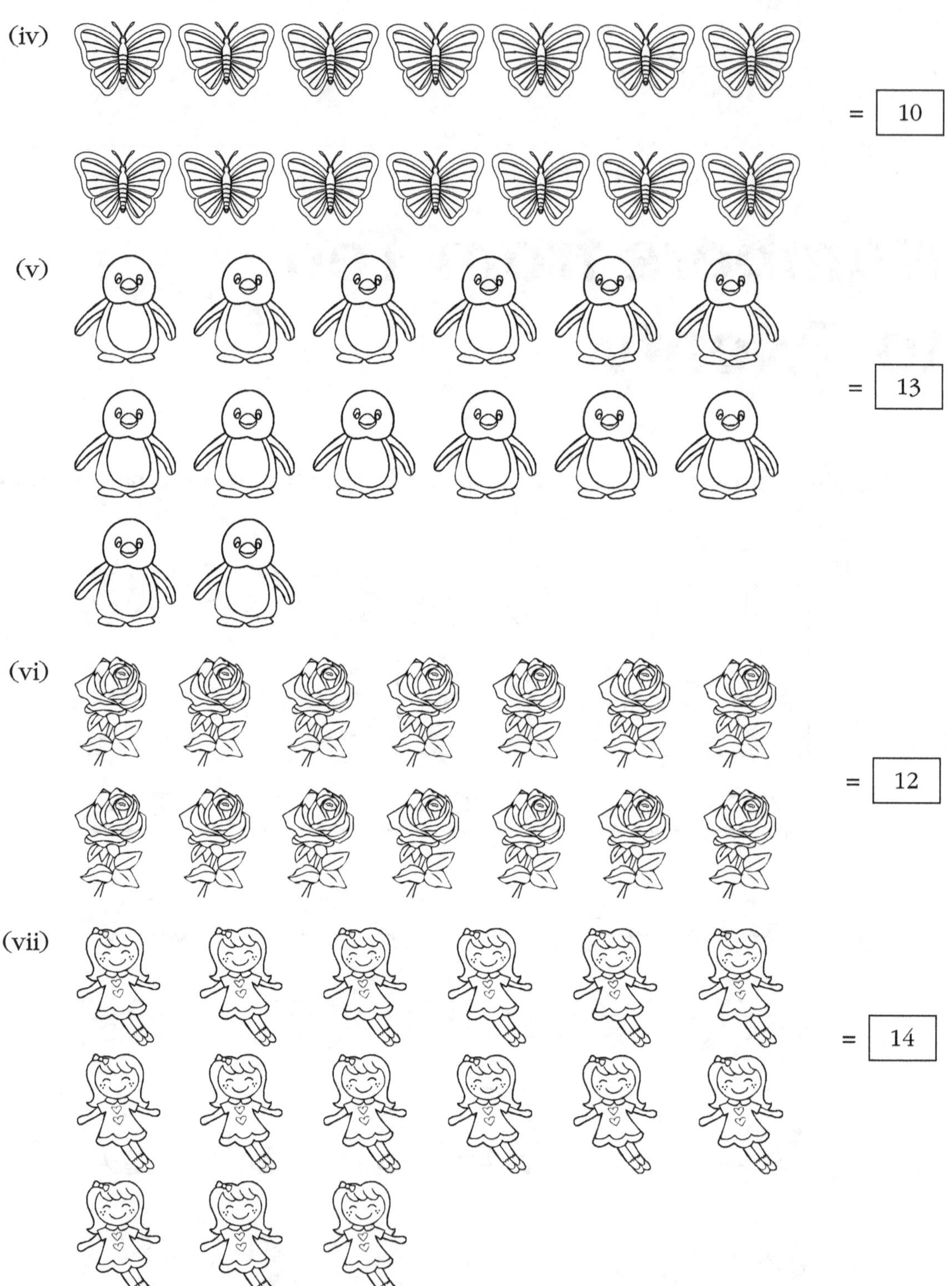

= 10

(v)

= 13

(vi)

= 12

(vii)

= 14

2 Make a group of 10 and write the numbers. One has been done for you.

(i)

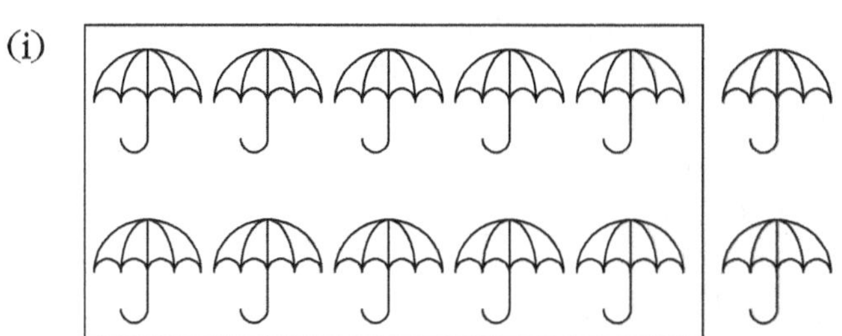

Tens	Ones
1	2

$$\boxed{10} + \boxed{2} = \boxed{12}$$

(ii)

Tens	Ones

$$\boxed{} + \boxed{} = \boxed{}$$

(iii)

Tens	Ones

$$\boxed{} + \boxed{} = \boxed{}$$

(iv)

Tens	Ones

$$\boxed{} + \boxed{} = \boxed{}$$

(v)

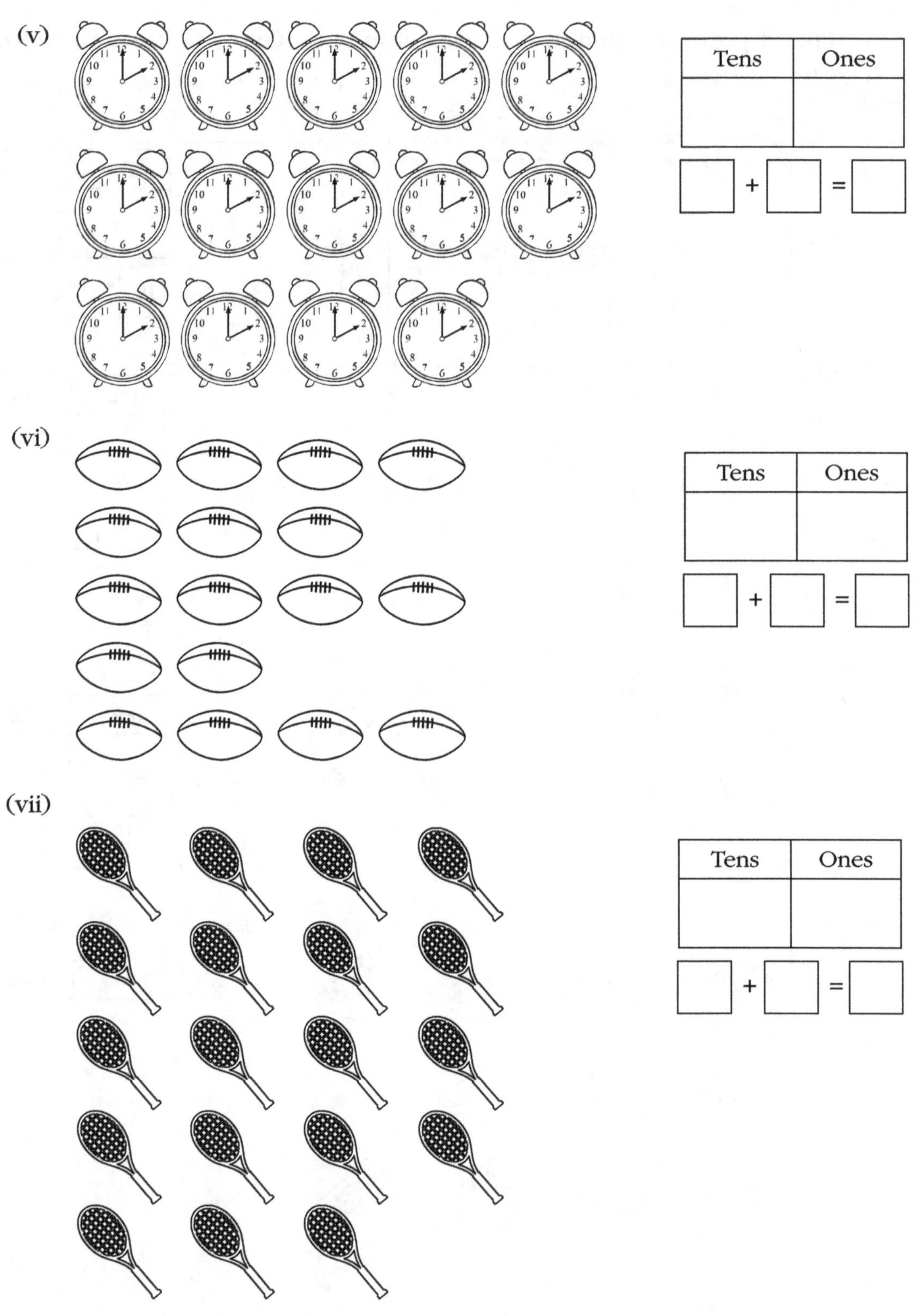

Tens	Ones

☐ + ☐ = ☐

(vi)

Tens	Ones

☐ + ☐ = ☐

(vii)

Tens	Ones

☐ + ☐ = ☐

3 Fill in the blanks. One has been done for you.

(i) 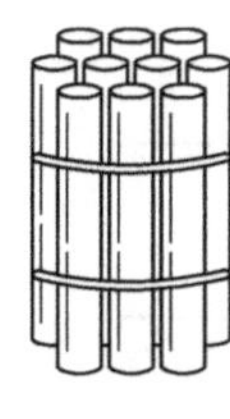 + 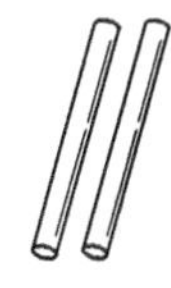 = 12

10   2

(ii) 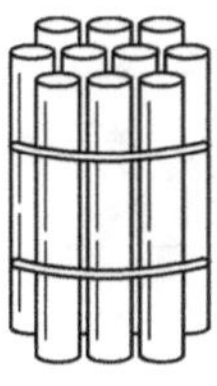 + 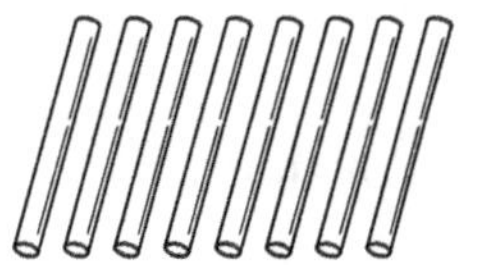 =

10   8

(iii) 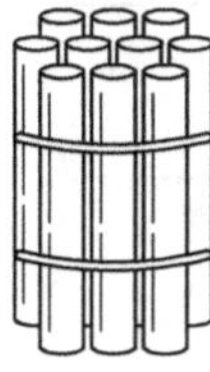 +  =

10   4

(iv) 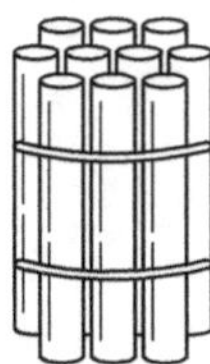 +  =

10   7

(v) 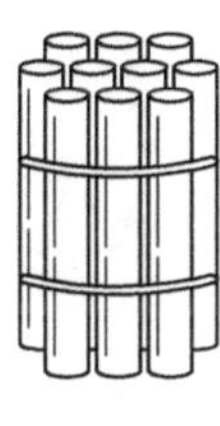 + 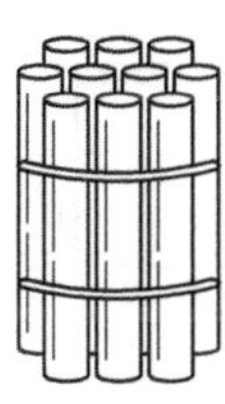 =

10   10

4 Write the next three numbers and their names.

(i) 10 _____ _____ _____   Ten   _____ _____ _____

(ii) 11 _____ _____ _____   Eleven   _____ _____ _____

(iii) 12 _____ _____ _____   Twelve   _____ _____ _____

(iv) 13 _____ _____ _____   Thirteen   _____ _____ _____

(v) 14 _____ _____ _____   Fourteen   _____ _____ _____

(vi) 15 _____ _____ _____   Fifteen   _____ _____ _____

(vii) 16 _____ _____ _____   Sixteen   _____ _____ _____

(viii) 17 _____ _____ _____   Seventeen   _____ _____ _____

5 Write the numbers before/after the given numbers.

(i)
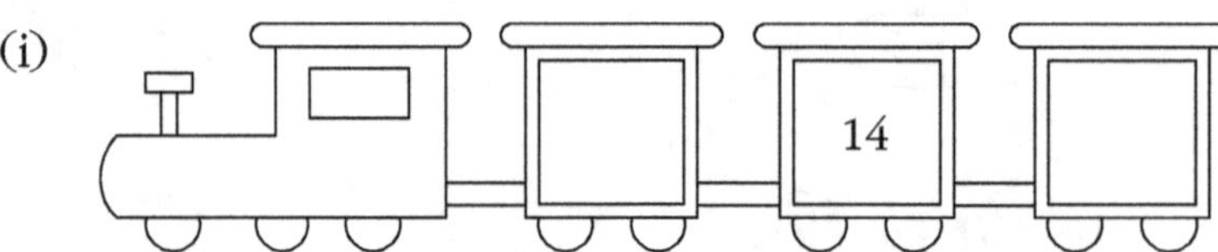

(ii)
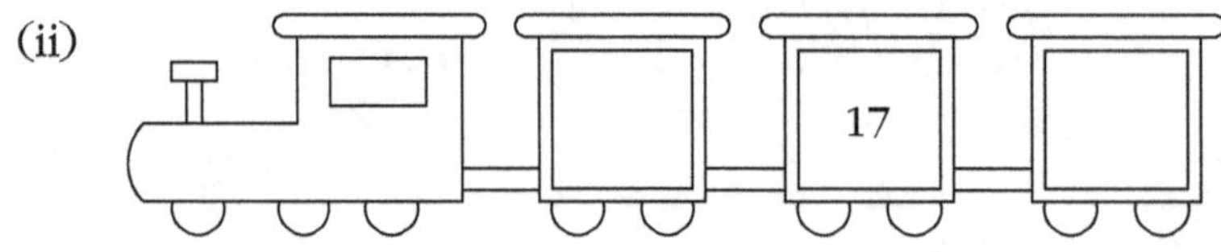

(iii)
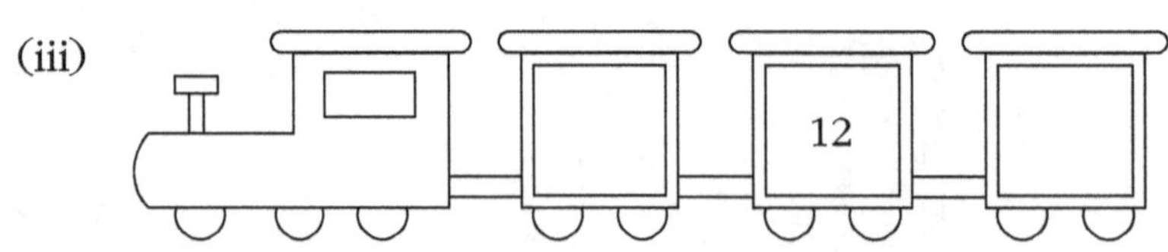

(iv)

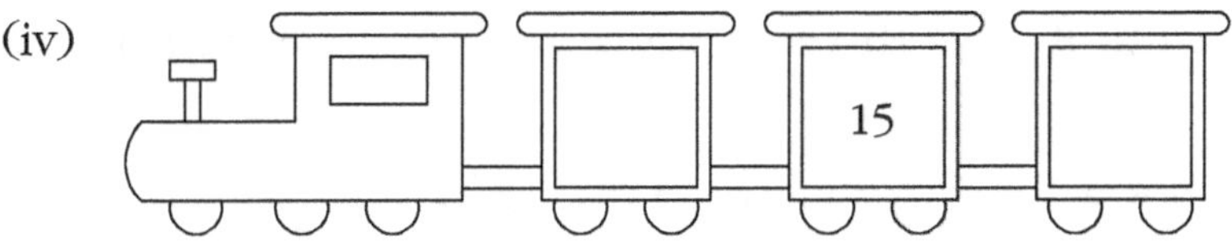

(v)

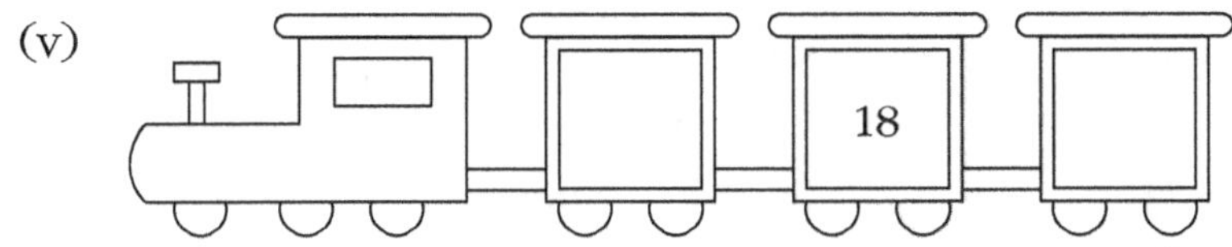

(vi)

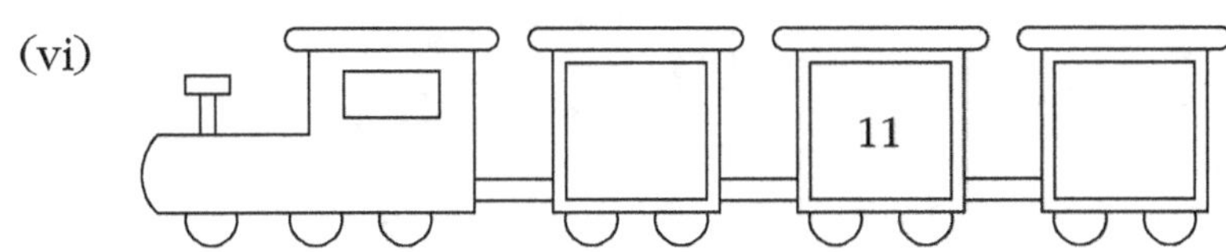

6 **Write the numbers between the given two numbers.**

(i)

(ii)

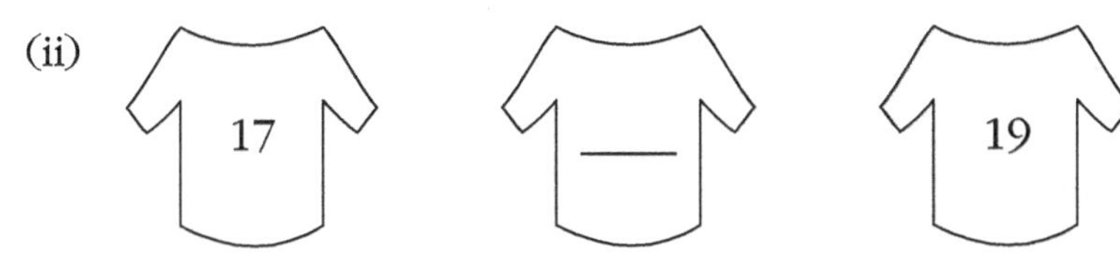

(iii)

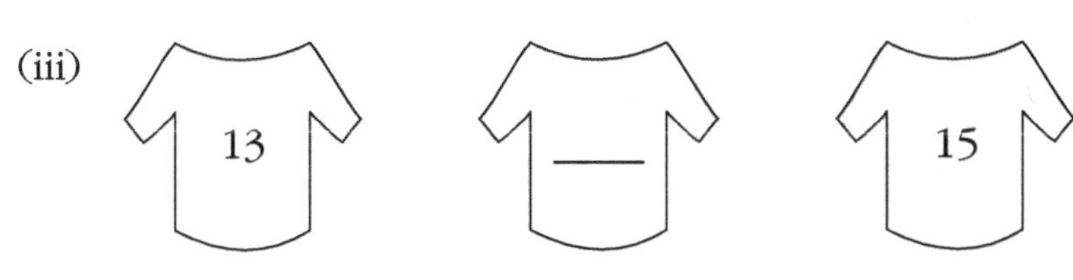

(iv)

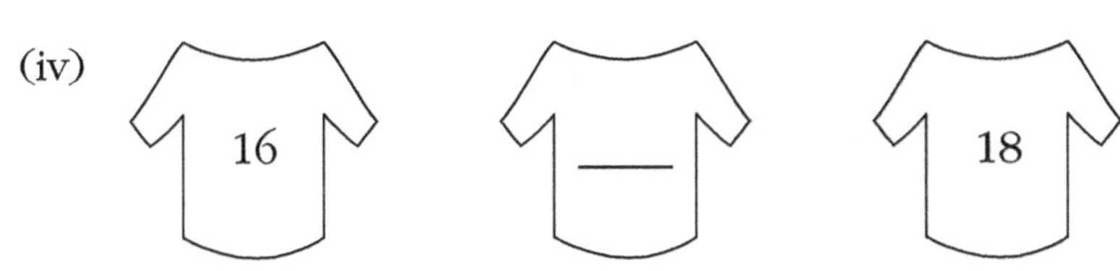

7 Circle the biggest number with red colour and smallest number with blue colour.

(i)

(ii)

(iii)

(iv)

(v)

(vi)
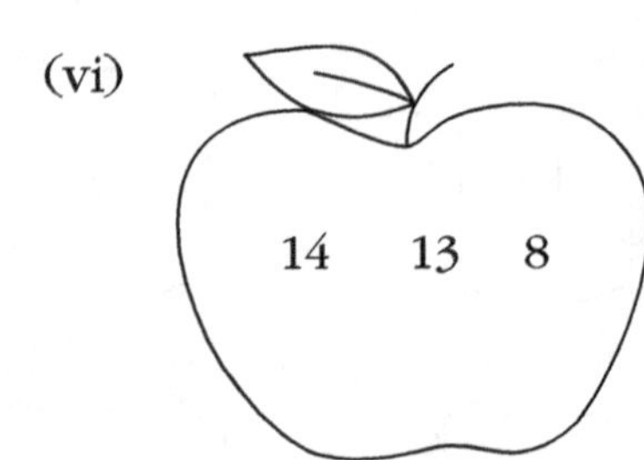

(vii)

(viii)
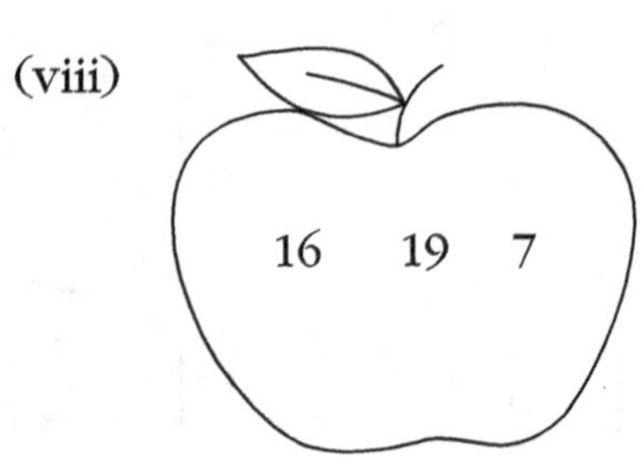

8 Add the following.

(i) $6 + 7$ = _____________   (ii) $8 + 6$ = _____________

(iii) $2 + 9$ = _____________   (iv) $12 + 4$ = _____________

(v) $17 + 2$ = _____________   (vi) $14 + 5$ = _____________

(vii) $18 + 2$ = _____________   (viii) $16 + 0$ = _____________

9 Solve these.

(i)	7 + 4	(ii)	12 + 7	(iii)	9 + 5
(iv)	13 + 6	(v)	15 + 2	(vi)	11 + 5
(vii)	12 + 6	(viii)	10 + 8	(ix)	16 + 1
(x)	11 + 4				

10 Solve these.

(i) 18 − 3 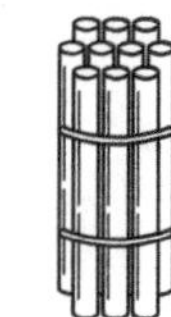 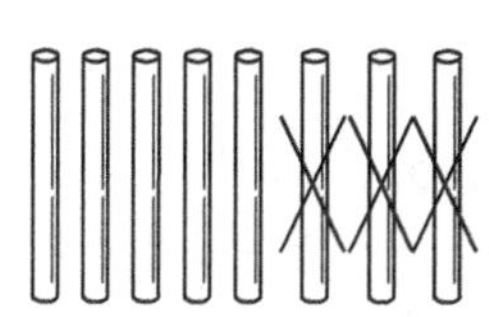

(ii) 17 − 3 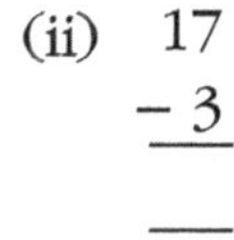 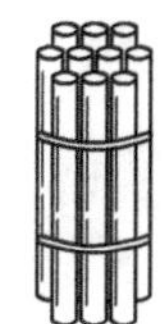 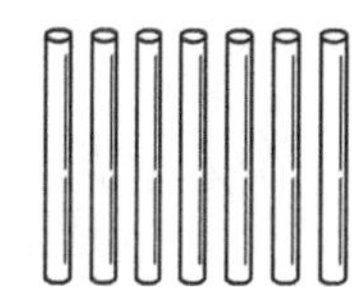

(iii) 18 − 5 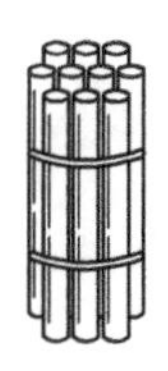 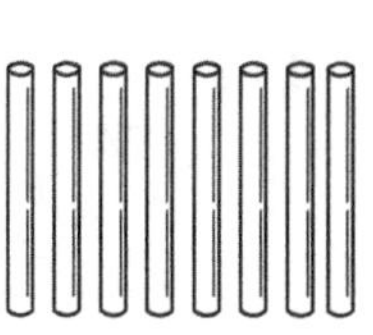

(iv) 19 − 8 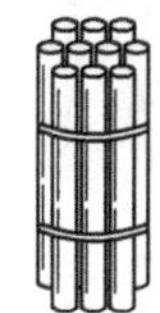 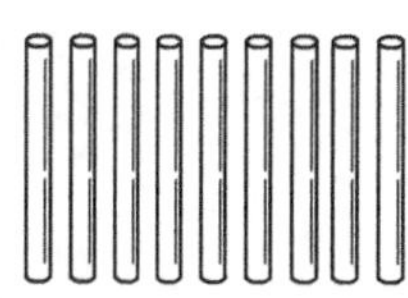

(v) 14 − 4 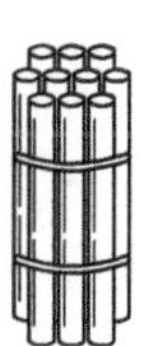 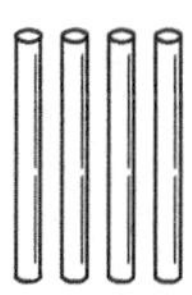

(vi) 15 − 4 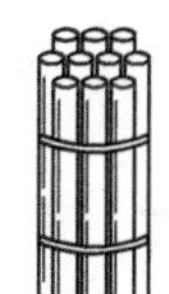 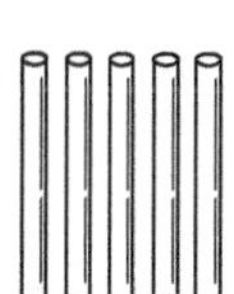

Time

1 **Fill in the blanks.**

Write M for Morning, A for Afternoon, E for Evening and N for Night.

(i) You eat dinner in the ☐

(ii) You get ready for bed in the ☐

(iii) You get out of school in the ☐

(iv) You eat breakfast in the ☐

(v) You go to school in the ☐

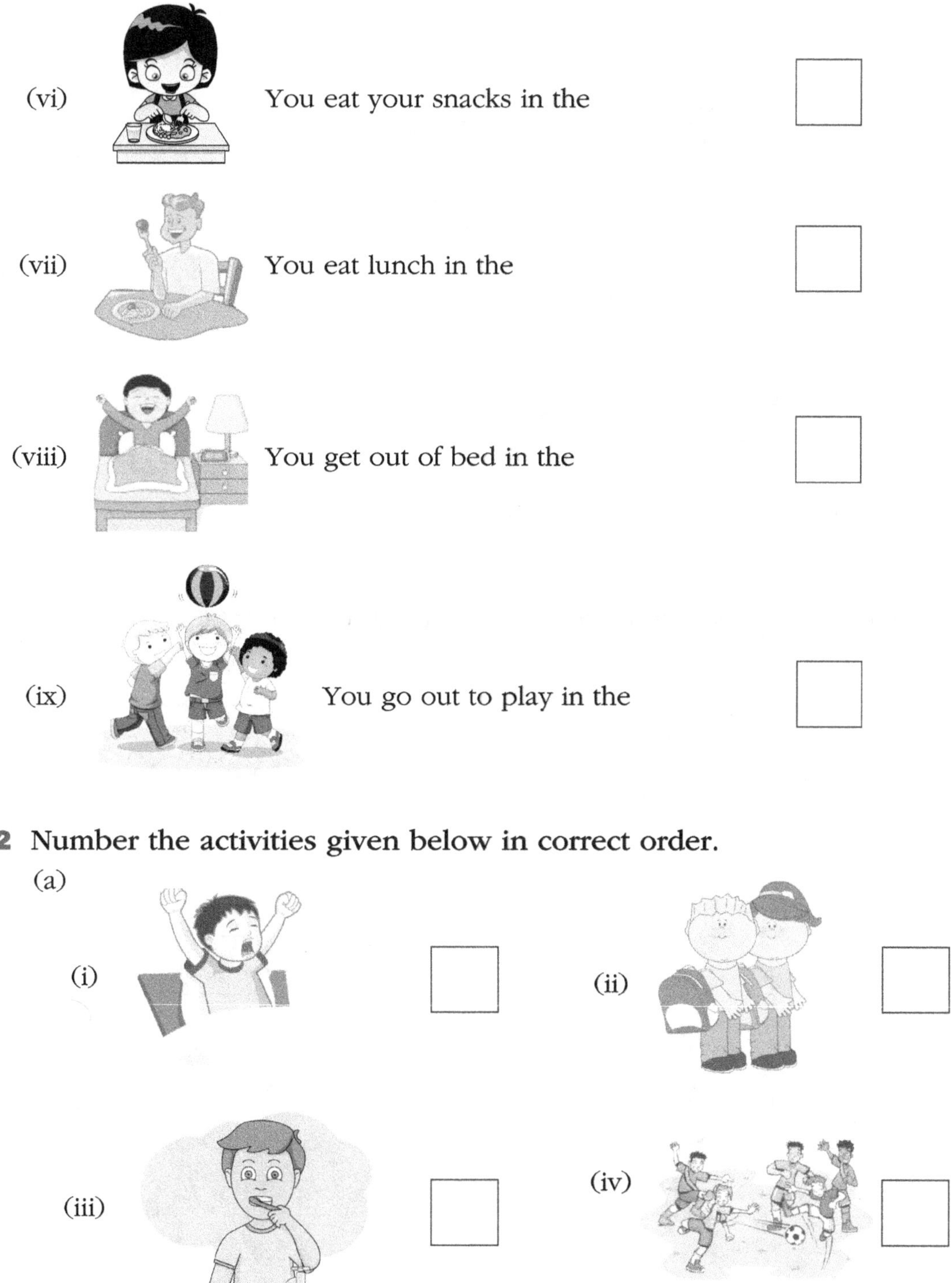

(vi) You eat your snacks in the ☐

(vii) You eat lunch in the ☐

(viii) You get out of bed in the ☐

(ix) You go out to play in the ☐

2 Number the activities given below in correct order.

(a)

(i) ☐   (ii) ☐

(iii) ☐   (iv) ☐

(b)

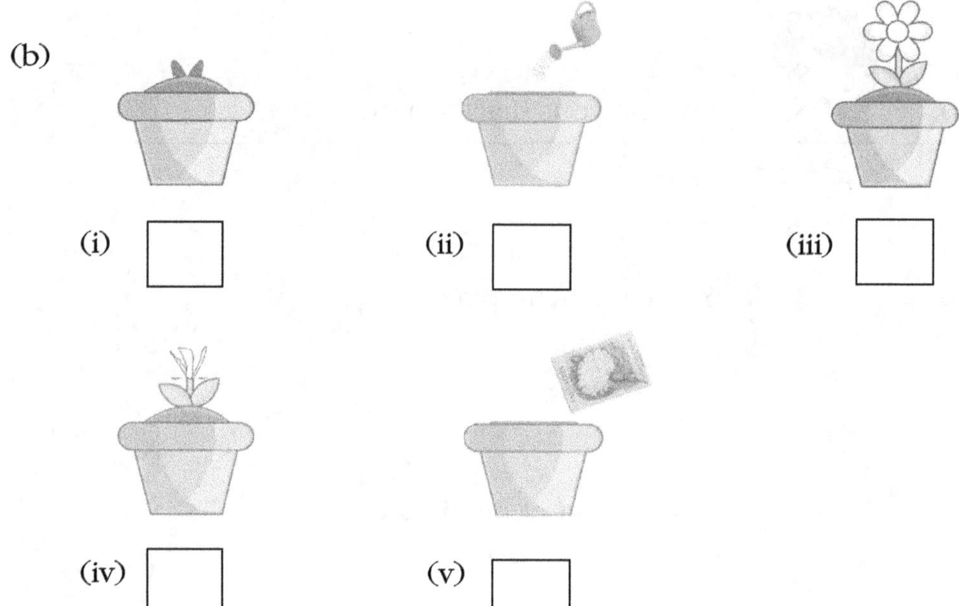

(i) ☐ (ii) ☐ (iii) ☐

(iv) ☐ (v) ☐

3 Tick (✓) the activity in each part that will take longer time.

(i)

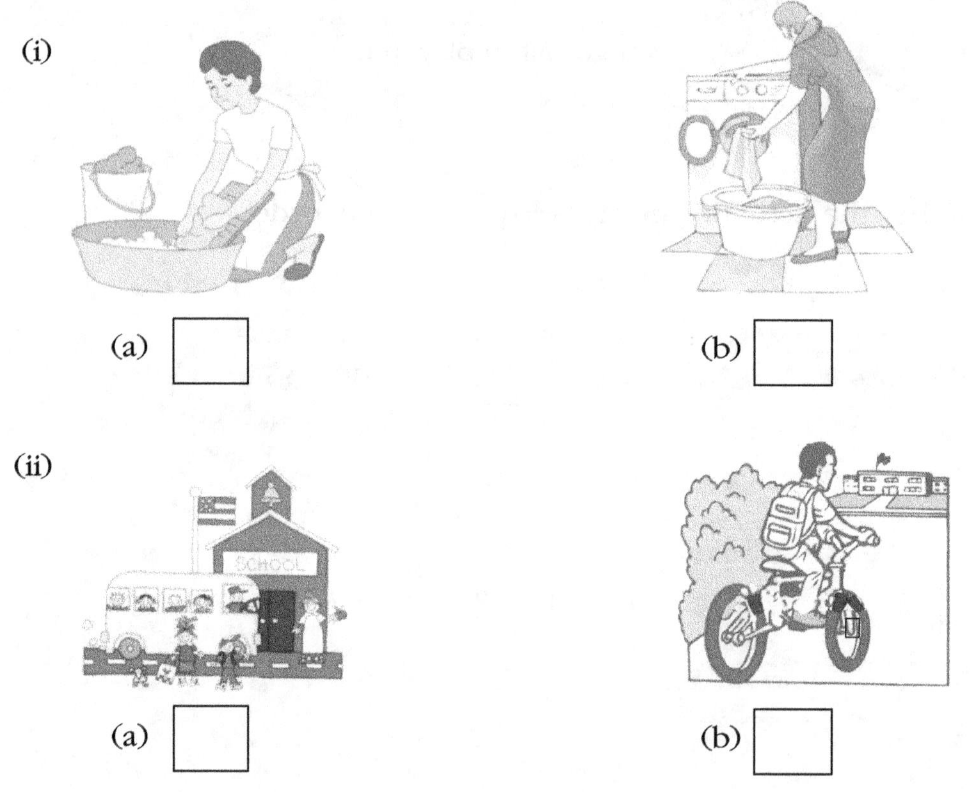

(a) ☐ (b) ☐

(ii)

(a) ☐ (b) ☐

Measurement

1 **Longer and Shorter.**

Tick (✓) the longer object and cross (✗) the shorter object.

(i) (a) [ ]   (b) [ ]

(ii) (a) [ ]   (b) [ ]

(iii) (a) [ ]   (b) [ ]

(iv) (a) [ ]   (b) [ ]

(v) (a) [ ]   (b) [ ]

2 **Longest and Shortest.**

(i) Tick (✓) the longest car.

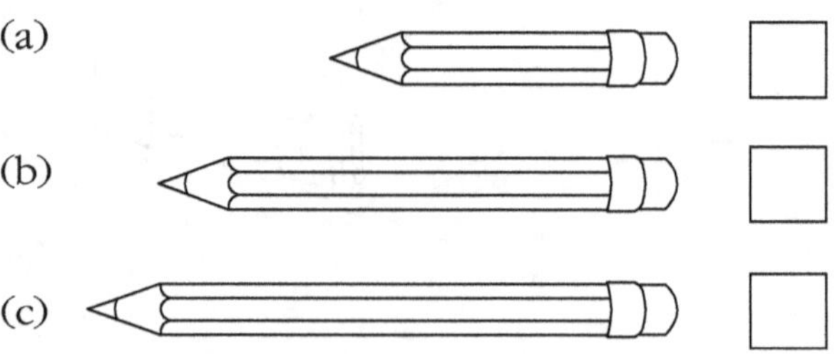

(a)   □   (b)   □   (c)   □

(ii) Tick (✓) the longest key.

(a)   □   (b)   □   (c)   □

(iii) Tick (✓) the shortest pencil.

(a)   □

(b)   □

(c)   □

(iv) Tick (✓) the longest truck.

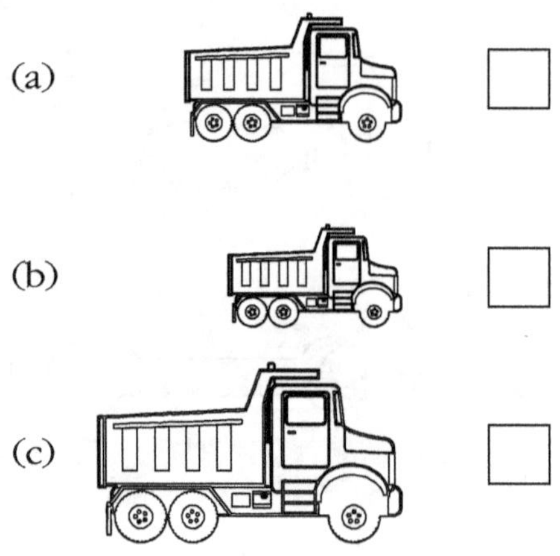

(a)   □

(b)   □

(c)   □

3 Taller and Shorter.

(i) Tick (✓) the taller building.

(a)  ☐

(b)  ☐

(ii) Tick (✓) the shorter table fan.

(a) 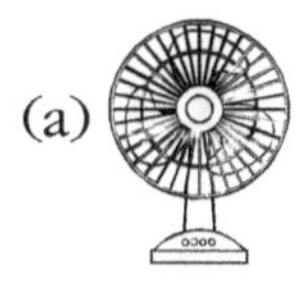 ☐

(b) 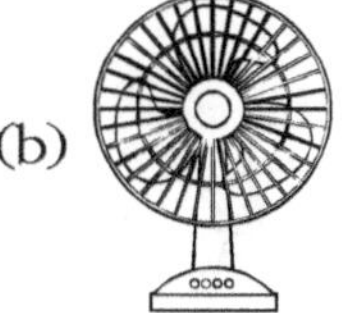 ☐

(iii) Tick (✓) the taller vase.

(a) 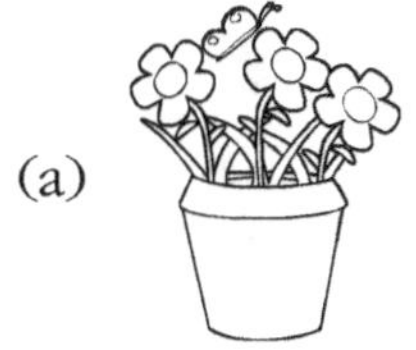 ☐

(b)  ☐

(iv) Tick (✓) the taller table.

(a) 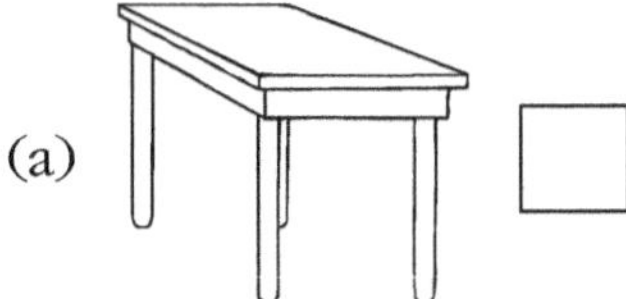 ☐

(b) 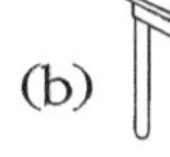 ☐

(v) Tick (✓) the shorter lamp.

(a) 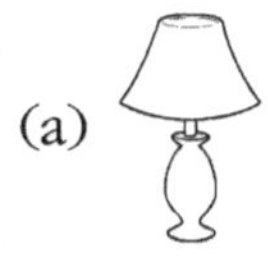 ☐

(b) 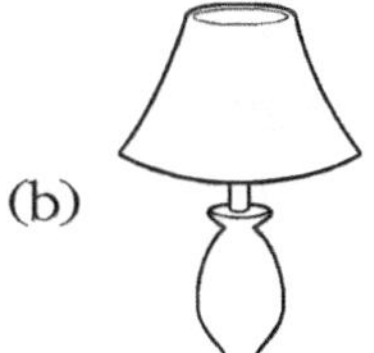 ☐

4 Tallest and Shortest.

(i) Tick (✓) the tallest object.

(ii) Tick (✓) the shortest table.

(iii) Tick (✓) the shortest animal.

(iv) Tick (✓) the tallest person.

5 Thicker and Thinner.

(i) Tick (✓) the thicker object.

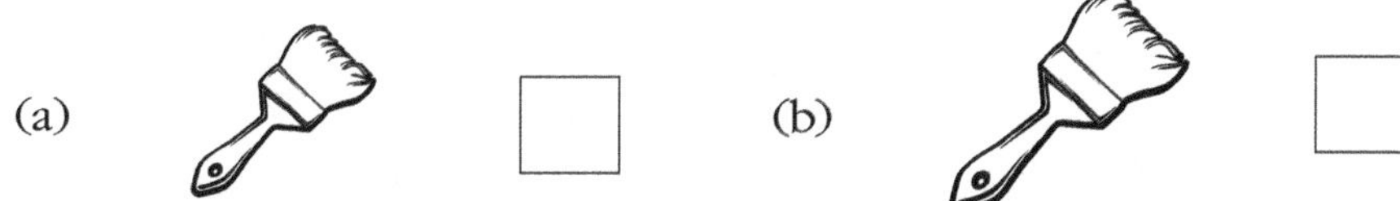

(a)　　　　　□　　　　(b)　　　　　□

(ii) Tick (✓) the thinner object.

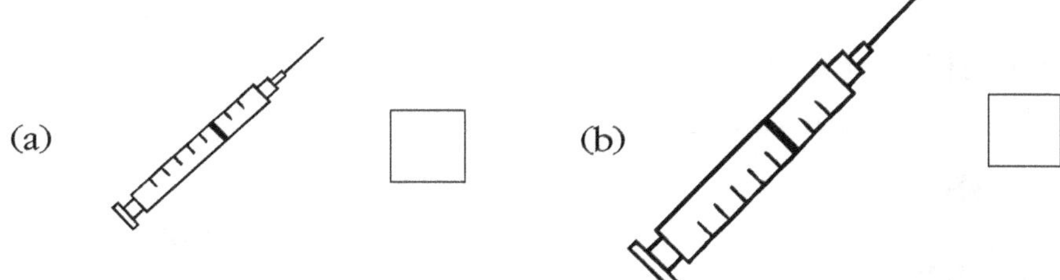

(a)　　　　　□　　　　(b)　　　　　□

(iii) Tick (✓) the thinner object.

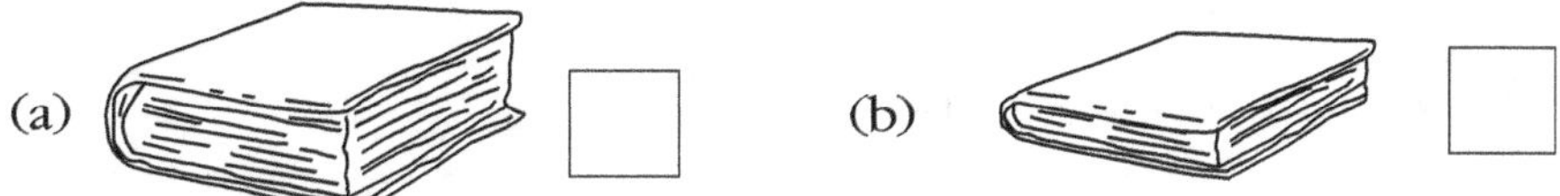

(a)　　　　　□　　　　(b)　　　　　□

(iv) Tick (✓) the thicker object.

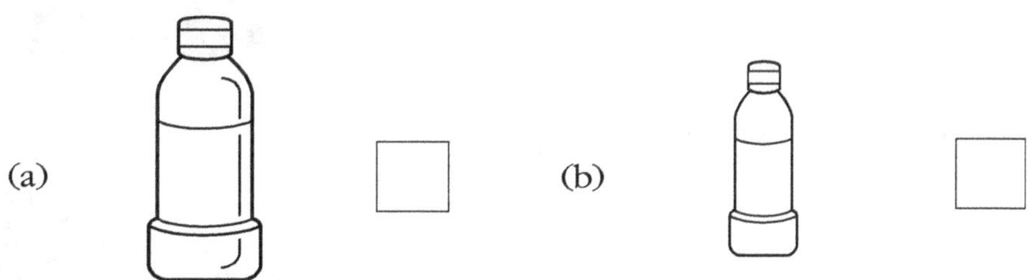

(a)　　　　　□　　　　(b)　　　　　□

6 Thickest and Thinnest.

(i) Tick (✓) the thickest object.

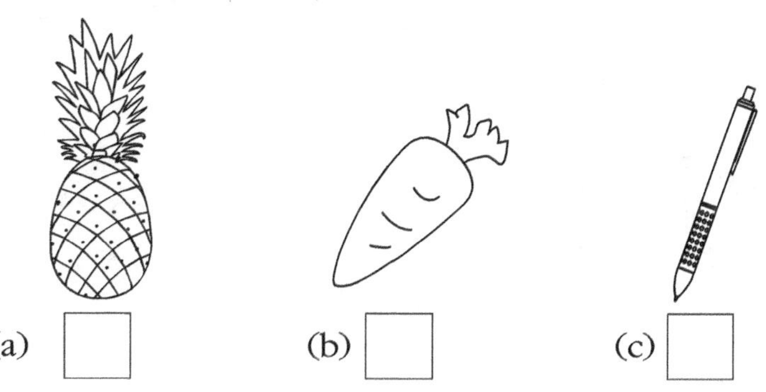

(a)　□　　　　(b)　□　　　　(c)　□

(ii) Tick (✓) the thinnest object.

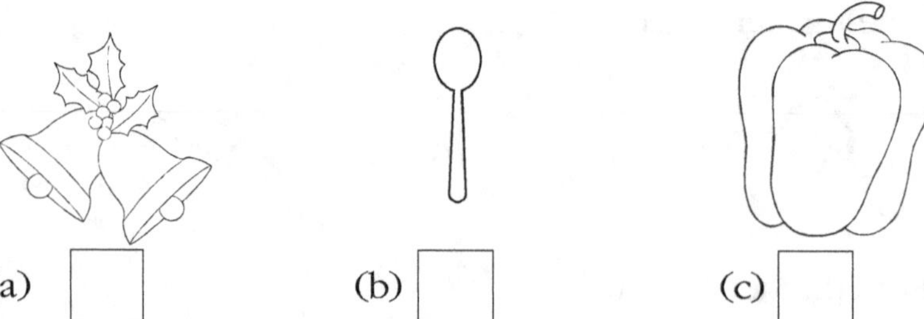

(a)   (b)   (c)

7 Heavier and Lighter.

(i) Tick (✓) the heavier animal.

(a)    (b)  

(ii) Tick (✓) the heavier vehicle.

(a)     (b)  

(iii) Tick (✓) the lighter animal.

(a)     (b) 

(iv) Tick (✓) the lighter object.

(a)  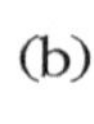   (b) 

8 Heaviest and Lightest.

(i) Tick (✓) the lightest object.

(a)  (b)  (c)

(ii) Tick (✓) the heaviest object.

(a)  (b)  (c)

(iii) Tick (✓) the heaviest object.

(a) 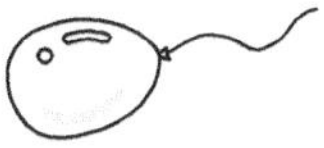 (b)  (c)

(iv) Tick (✓) the lightest object.

(a)  (b) 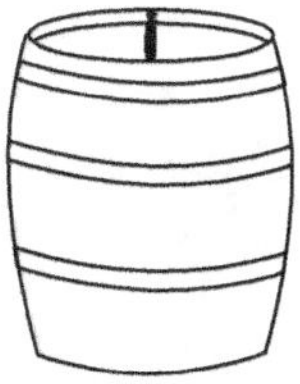 (c)

Chapter 8

Numbers from Twenty-one to Fifty

1 Write the number. One has been done for you.

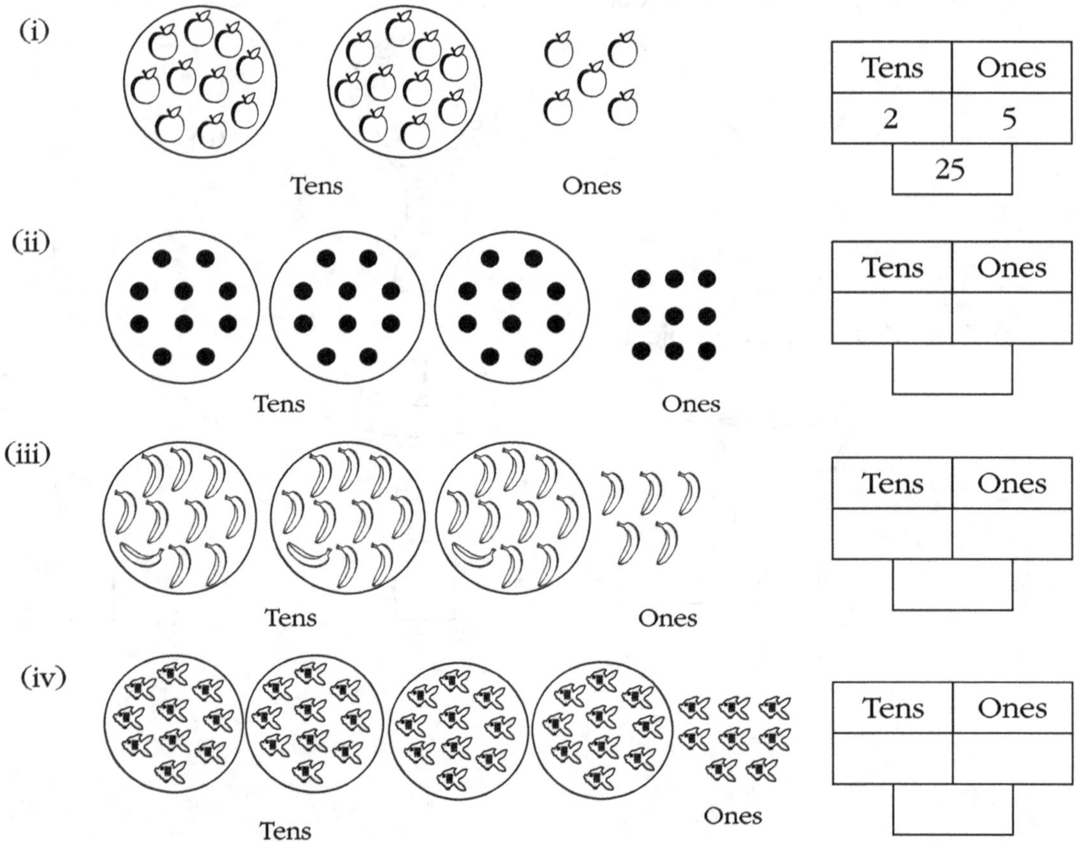

2 Fill in the boxes. One has been done for you.

(i)

Tens	Ones
2	7

= 27

(ii)

Tens	Ones
3	0

=

(iii)

Tens	Ones
3	1

=

(iv)

Tens	Ones
3	9

=

(v)

Tens	Ones
4	5

=

(vi)

Tens	Ones
4	8

=

3 Draw and fill in the boxes (numbers from 41 to 50). One has been done for you.

(i)

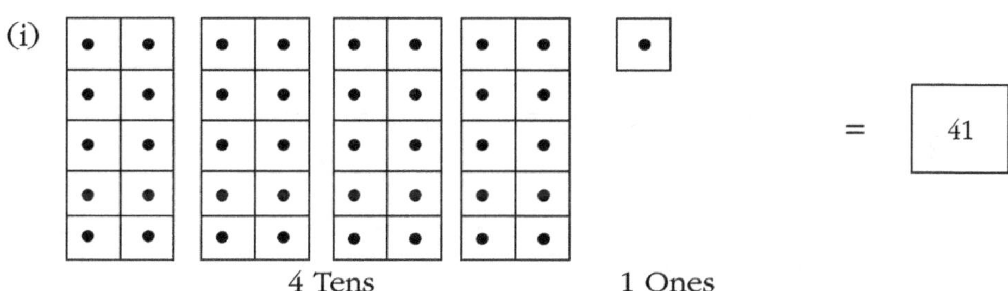

4 Tens   1 Ones   = 41

(ii)

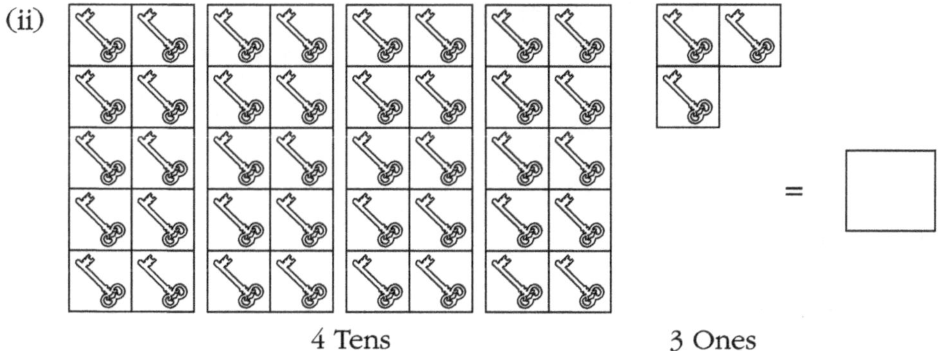

4 Tens   3 Ones   =

(iii) 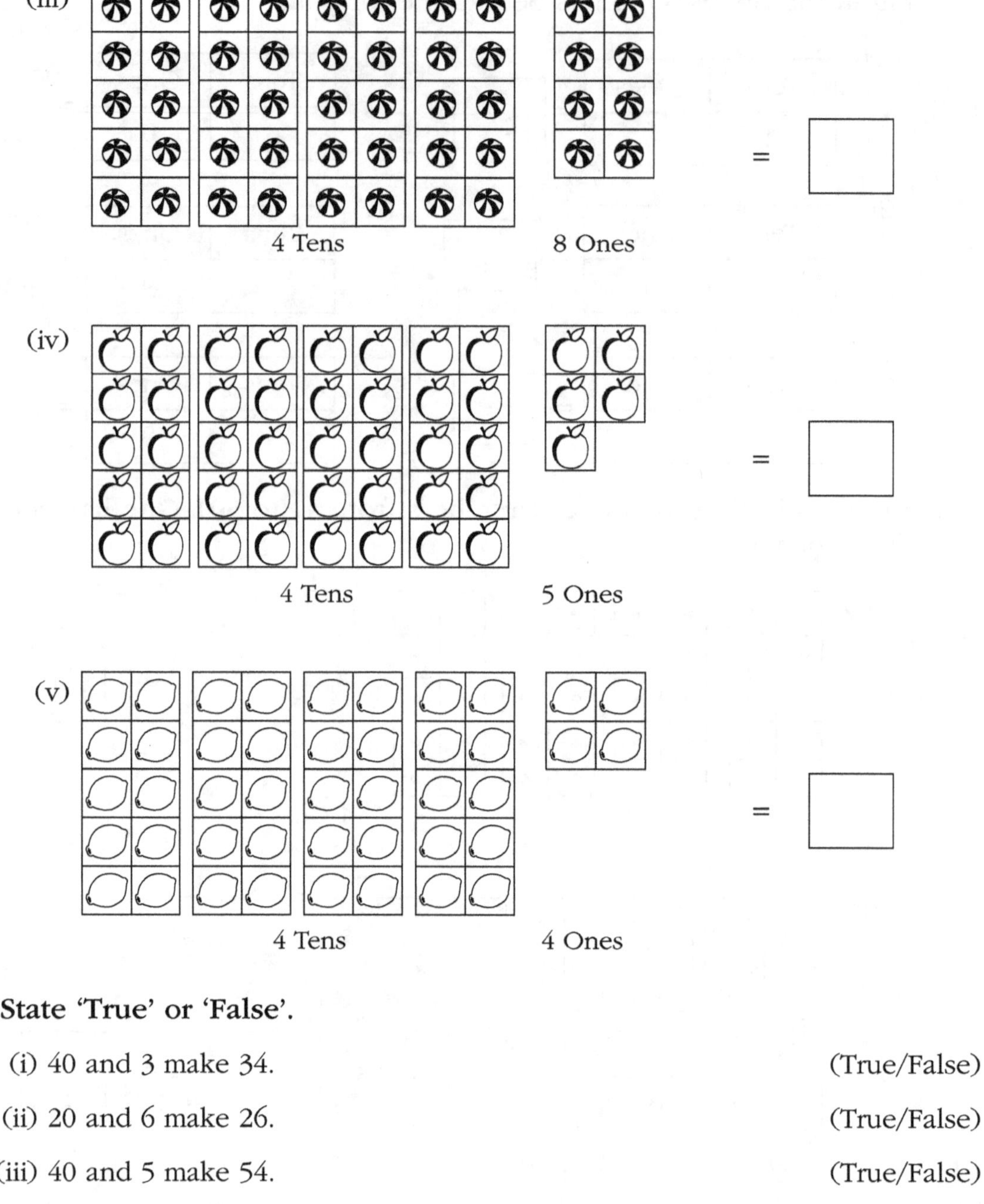

4 Tens   8 Ones   =

(iv)

4 Tens   5 Ones   =

(v)

4 Tens   4 Ones   =

4 State 'True' or 'False'.

  (i) 40 and 3 make 34.   (True/False)

 (ii) 20 and 6 make 26.   (True/False)

(iii) 40 and 5 make 54.   (True/False)

(iv) 20 and 9 make 29.   (True/False)

 (v) 30 and 7 make 47.   (True/False)

Chapter 9

Data Handling

1 Look at the picture given below.

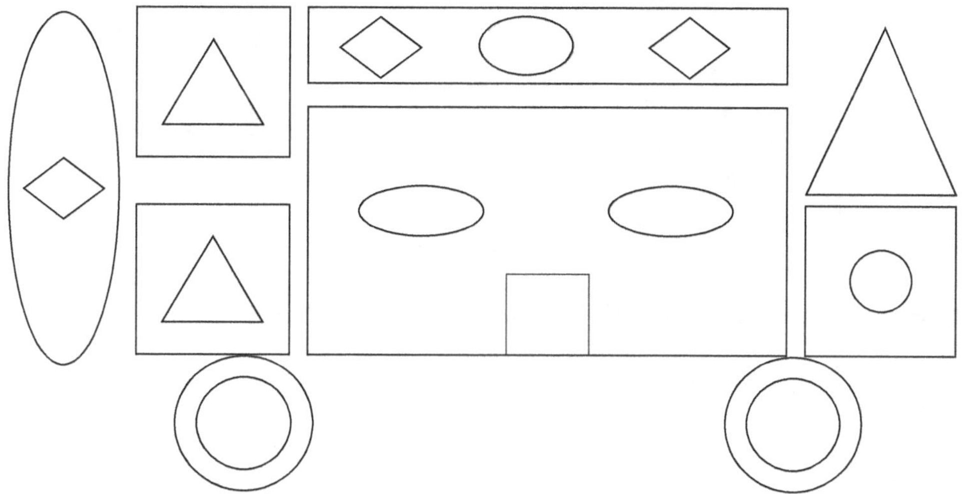

Count the shapes in the above picture.

(i) ⬜ = ☁   (ii) △ = ☁

(iii) ▭ = ☁   (iv) ◯ = ☁

(v) ⬭ = ☁   (vi) ◇ = ☁

2 Look at the picture given below.

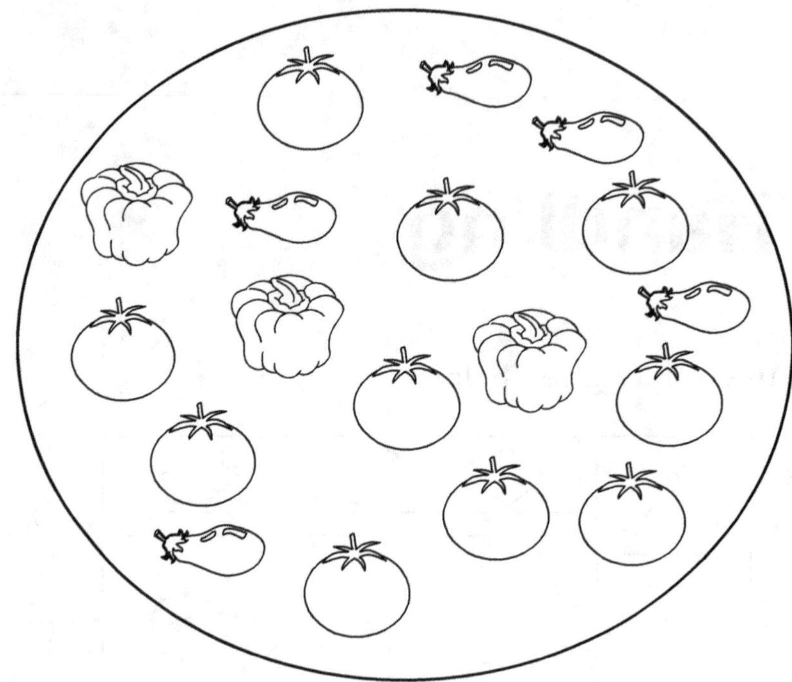

State 'True' or 'False' on the basis of above picture.

(i)   Number of ⬤ = 12 [ ]

(ii)   Number of 🍆 = 5 [ ]

(iii) Number of 🫑 = 3 [ ]

3 **Given below are the names of vegetables.**

(i) Count the number of letters in each name (word). One has been done for you.

	Name		Number of letters

Name   **Number of letters**

(a) T O M A T O   6

(b) B R I N J A L

(c) O N I O N

(d) C A R R O T

(e) C A B B A G E

(f) C U C U M B E R

(ii) How many names have six letters?

(iii) How many names have five letters?

(iv) How many names have seven letters?

(v) How many times (A) comes in all the names together?

(vi) How many times (O) comes in all the names together?

(vii) How many times (I) comes in all the names together?

Chapter 10

Patterns

1 Extend the sequence in the same pattern that follows.

(i)

(ii)

(iii)

(iv)

(v)

2 Complete the pattern.

(i)

(ii)

(iii)

(iv)

3 Fill in the boxes to complete the sequence.

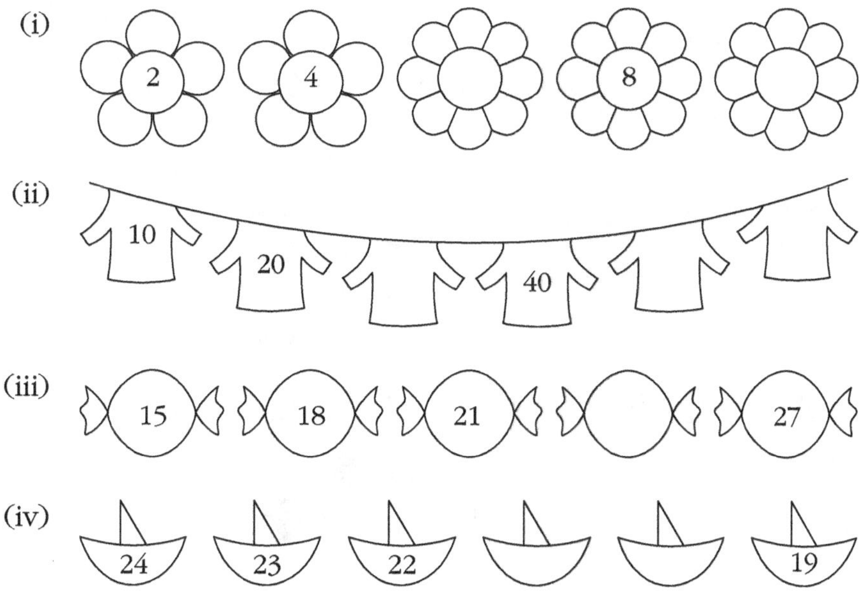

4 Study the pattern and fill in the missing numbers.

(i)

(ii)

(iii)

(iv)

5 Complete the pattern.

(i)

(ii)

(iii)

(iv)

6 Choose the correct pattern that comes next.

(i)

   (a)

   (b)

   (c)

(ii)

   (a)

   (b)

   (c)

(iii)

   (a)

   (b)

   (c)

(iv)

   (a)

   (b)

   (c)

Numbers

1 Draw the circles as per the given numbers. One has been done for you.

(i)

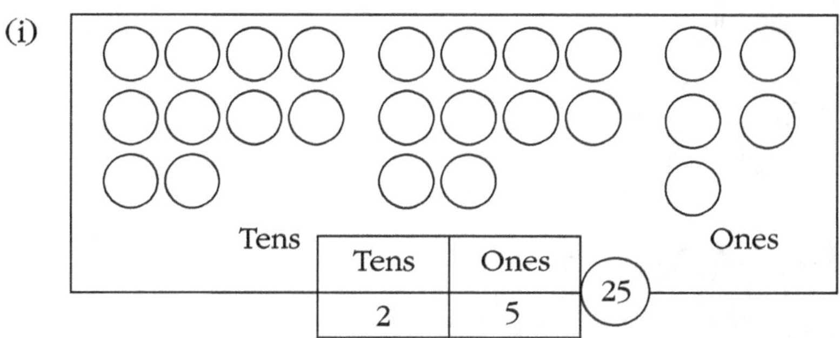

(ii)

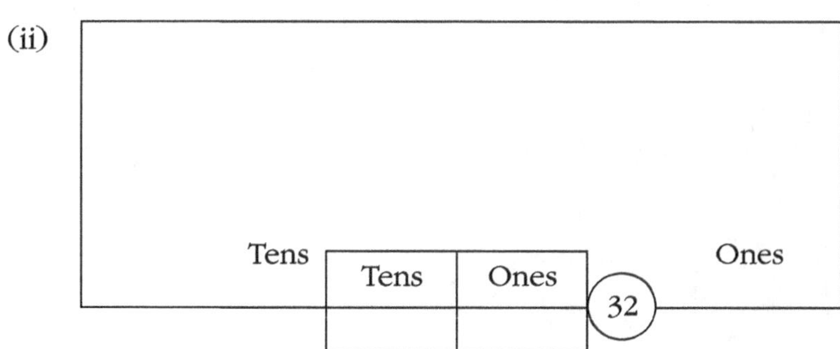

(iii)

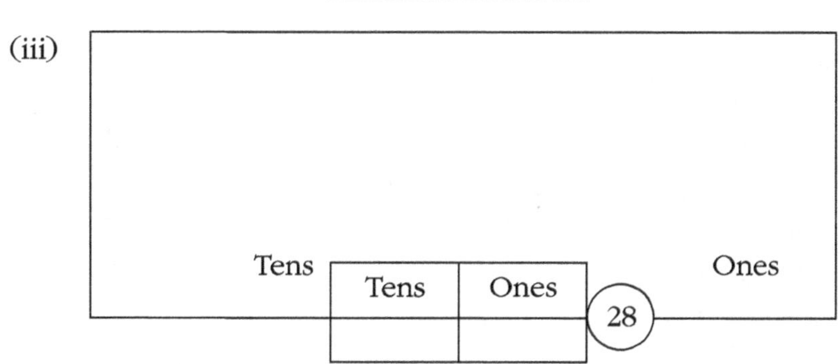

(i) 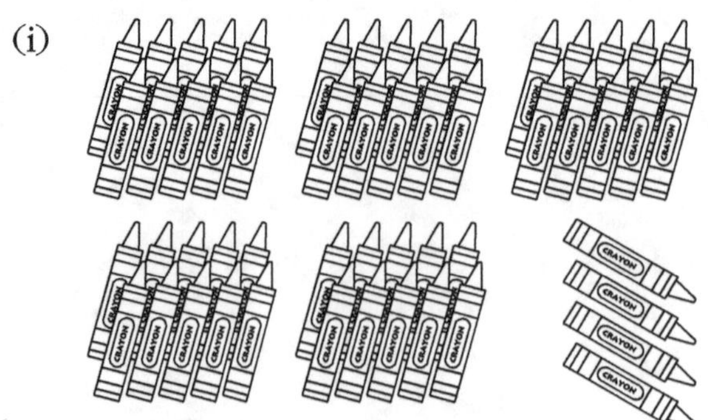

Tens	Ones
5	4

54

(ii) 

Tens	Ones

(iii) 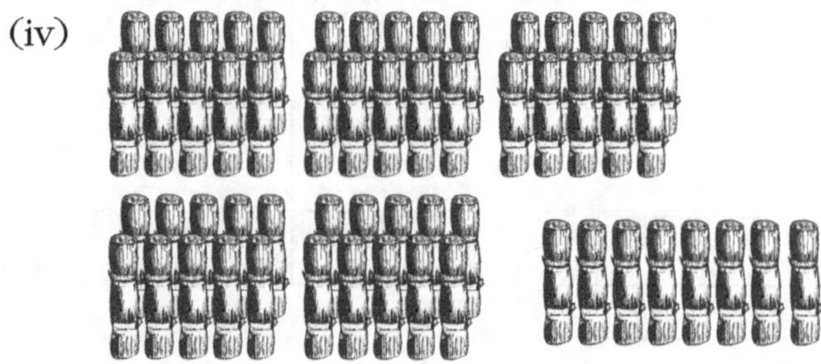

Tens	Ones

(iv) 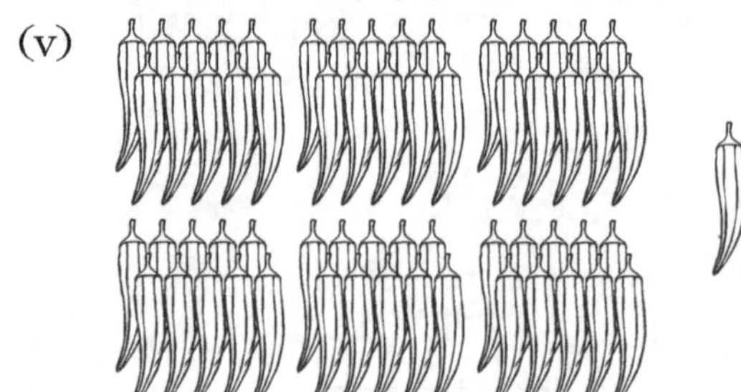

Tens	Ones

(v)

Tens	Ones

3 Fill in the boxes. One has been done for you.

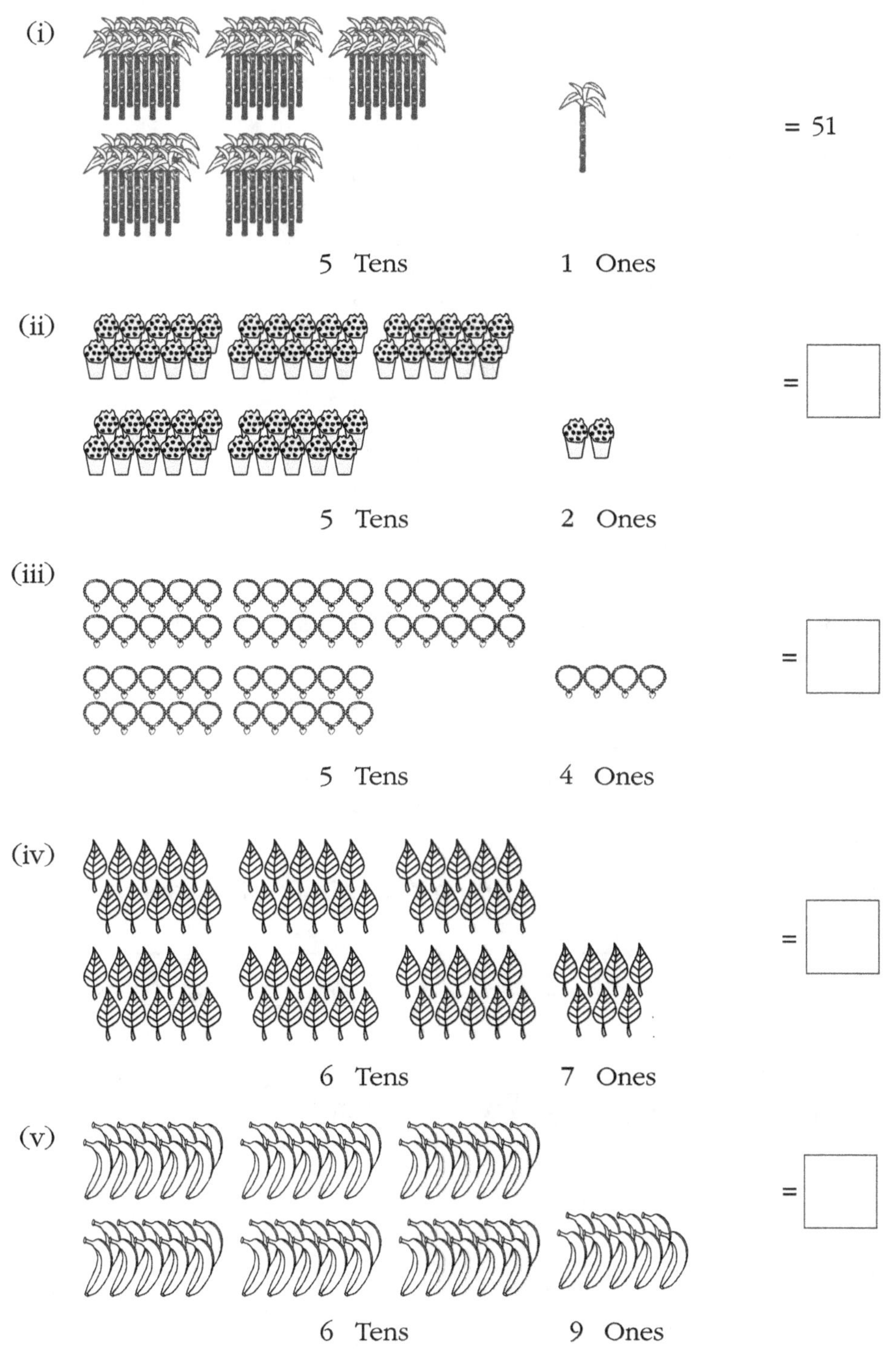

(i)
5 Tens   1 Ones   = 51

(ii)
5 Tens   2 Ones   =

(iii)
5 Tens   4 Ones   =

(iv)
6 Tens   7 Ones   =

(v)
6 Tens   9 Ones   =

4 Write the following numerals as tens and ones. One has been done for
you.

(i) 64 = **6** tens   **4** ones

(ii) 76 = ☐ tens   ☐ ones

(iii) 51 = ☐ tens   ☐ ones

(iv) 82 = ☐ tens   ☐ ones

(v) 96 = ☐ tens   ☐ ones

(vi) 59 = ☐ tens   ☐ ones

(vii) 65 = ☐ tens   ☐ ones

(viii) 84 = ☐ tens   ☐ ones

(ix) 75 = ☐ tens   ☐ ones

(x) 66 = ☐ tens   ☐ ones

5 Complete the sequence by filling the missing numbers.

(i) 
76, 77, ☐, ☐, 80, ☐

(ii) 62, ☐, ☐, 65, ☐, 67

(iii) ☐, 54, ☐, ☐, 57, ☐

(iv)

(v)

(vi)

(vii)

Chapter 12

Money

1 Match the rupees and coins with correct values. One has been done for you.

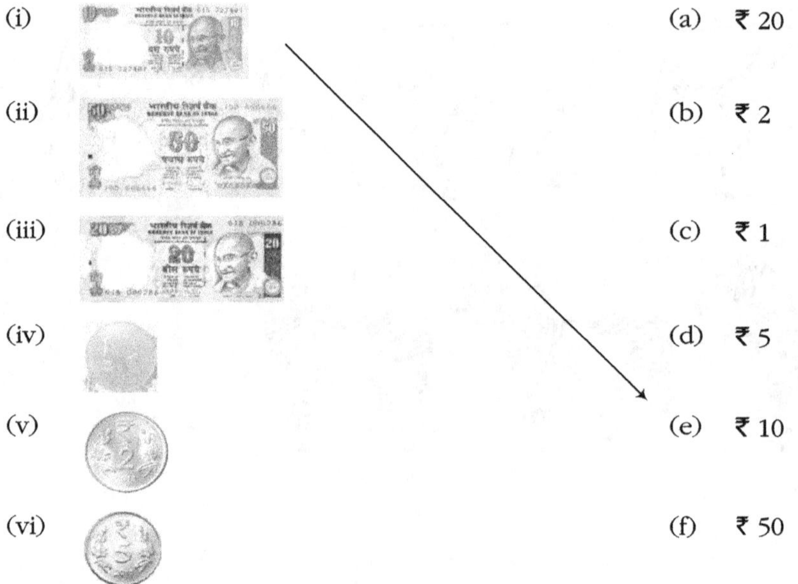

(i)   (a) ₹ 20

(ii)   (b) ₹ 2

(iii) (c) ₹ 1

(iv)   (d) ₹ 5

(v)   (e) ₹ 10

(vi)   (f) ₹ 50

2 (i) Make the given amount using different possible combinations of coins.

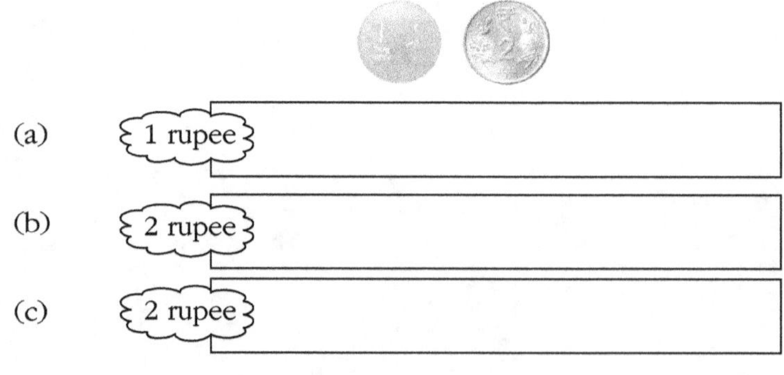

(a)

(b)

(c)

(d) ⟨3 rupee⟩

(e) ⟨3 rupee⟩

(ii) Make the given amount using different possible combination of coins.

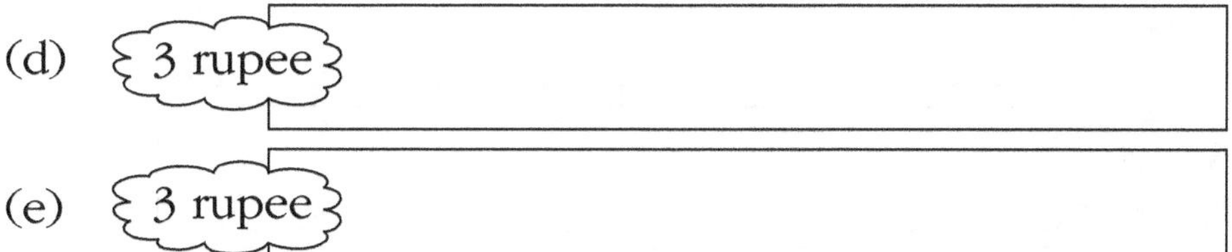

(a) ⟨4 rupee⟩

(b) ⟨4 rupee⟩

(c) ⟨4 rupee⟩

(d) ⟨5 rupee⟩

(e) ⟨5 rupee⟩

(f) ⟨5 rupee⟩

(g) ⟨5 rupee⟩

3 Count and write the total amount of money. One has been done for you.

(i)  = ₹ 18

(ii)  = ___________

(iii) = ___________

(iv) = ___________

4 Count the total amount of money and mark (✓), if you can buy the object and mark (✗), if you can't buy the object.

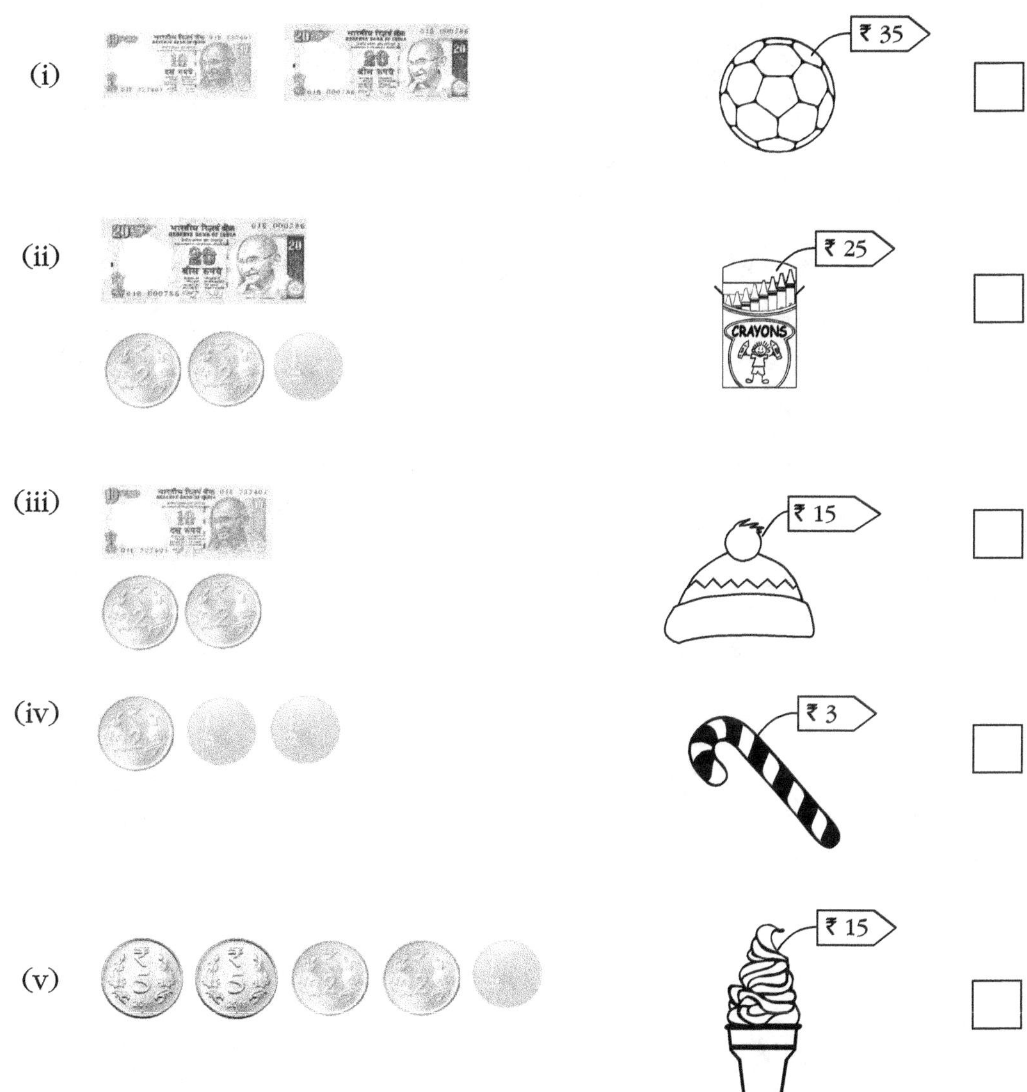

5 Guess and match the items with the correct amount. One has been done for you.

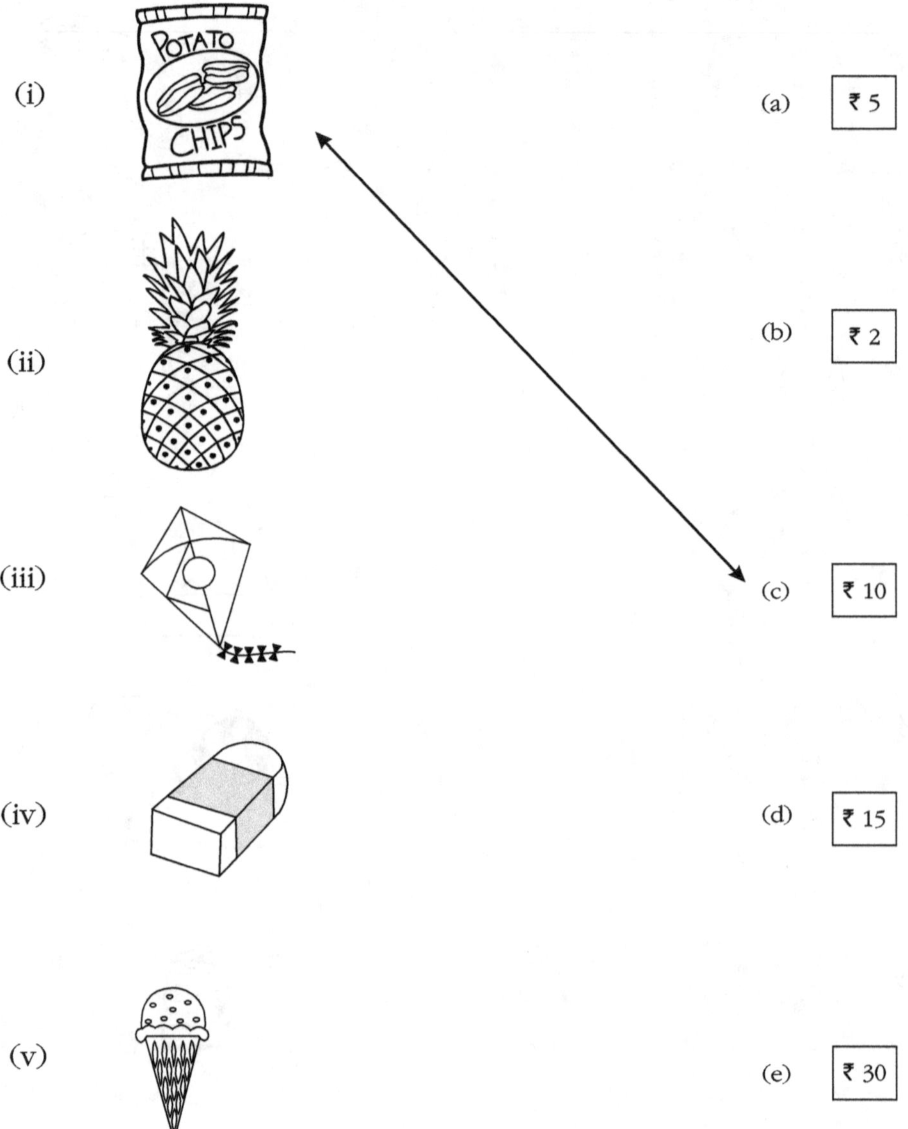

Chapter 13

How Many

1 Write the number of objects.

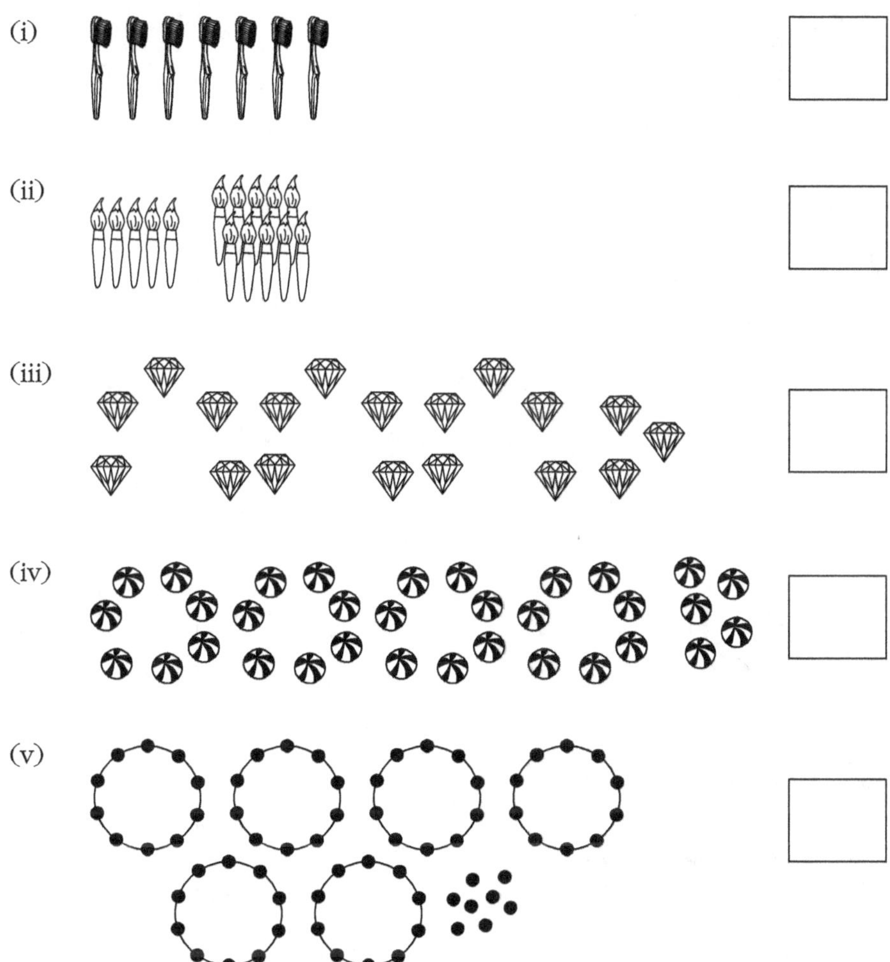

(i)

(ii)

(iii)

(iv)

(v)

(vi) 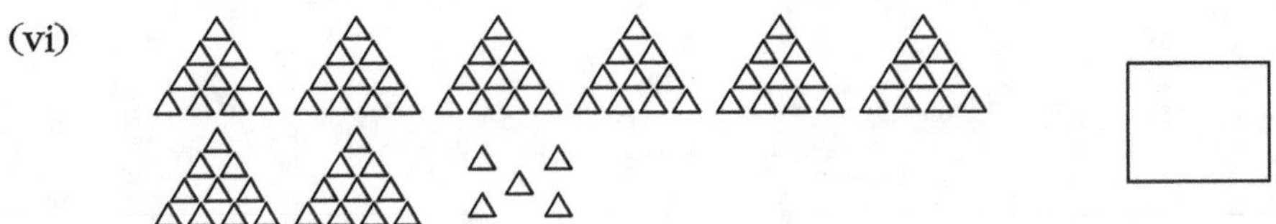

2 How much will the following cost?

(i) 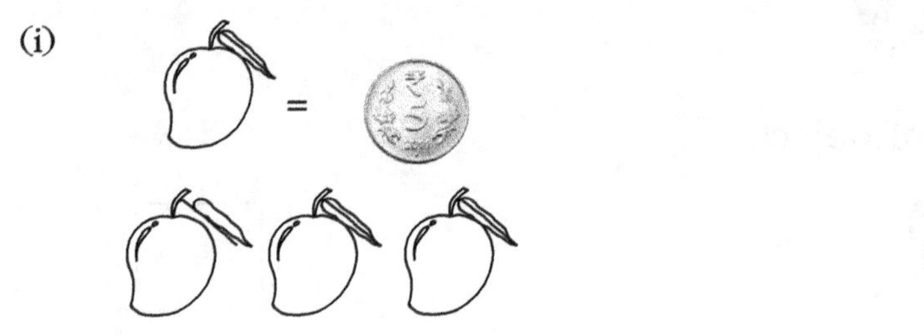

(ii) 

(iii)

(iv)

3 Write the number name.

	Number	Number name		Number	Number name
(i)	16		(iv)	29	
(ii)	23		(v)	36	
(iii)	19		(vi)	31	

4 How many tens and ones? One has been done for you.

(i) 23 = [2] tens [3] ones   (ii) 46 = [ ] tens [ ] ones

(iii) 75 = [ ] tens [ ] ones   (iv) 24 = [ ] tens [ ] ones

(v) 39 = [ ] tens [ ] ones   (vi) 62 = [ ] tens [ ] ones

(vii) 81 = [ ] tens [ ] ones   (viii) 96 = [ ] tens [ ] ones

(ix) 43 = [ ] tens [ ] ones   (x) 51 = [ ] tens [ ] ones

5 Circle the bigger number and cross out the smaller number.

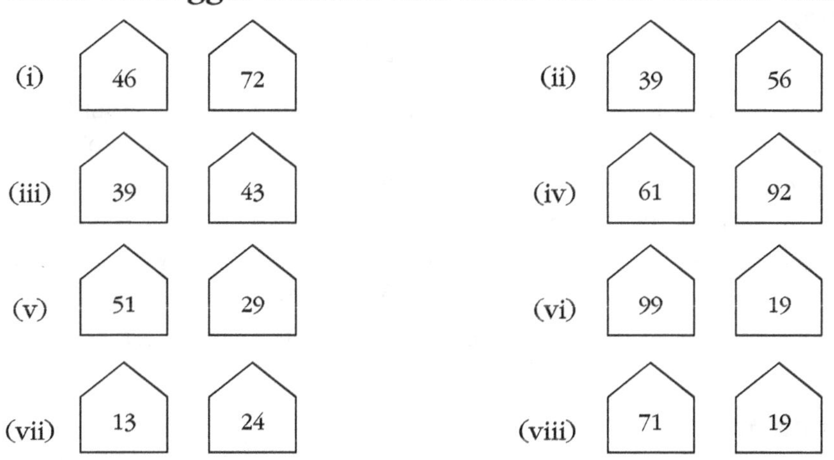

Answers

Chapter 1 Shapes and Space

1. (i) (a) ✓ (b) ✗ (ii) (a) ✗ (b) ✓
(iii) (a) ✓ (b) ✗ (iv) (a) ✓ (b) ✗

3. (i) (a) ✓ (b) ✗ (ii) (a) ✓ (c) ✗
(iii) (a) ✗ (c) ✓ (iv) (a) ✓ (c) ✗

6. (i) (a) (ii) (a) (iii) (c) (iv) (a)

7. (i) above (ii) on (iii) on
(iv) above (v) above (vi) on

8. (i) (b) ✗ (c) ✓ (ii) (a) ✗ (c) ✓
(iii) (a) ✓ (b) ✗ (iv) (b) ✓ (c) ✗

10. (i) (b) (ii) (c)
(iii) (a) (iv) (e) (v) (d)

Chapter 2 Numbers from One to Nine

2. (i) 1 (ii) 5 (iii) 2 (iv) 7
(v) 6 (vi) 3 (vii) 9 (viii) 4

3. (i) (a) ✗ (b) ✓ (ii) (a) ✗ (b) ✓
(iii) (a) ✓ (b) ✗ (iv) (a) ✗ (b) ✓
(v) (a) ✓ (b) ✗

4. (i)–(c), (ii)–(d), (iii)–(b),
(iv)–(e), (v)–(a)

6. (i)–(d), (ii)–(e), (iii)–(f), (iv)–(g),
(v)–(c), (vi)–(h), (vii)–(b), (viii)–(a)

8. (i) 9 (ii) 5 (iii) 4 (iv) 7

9. (i) 4 (ii) 8 (iii) 6 (iv) 5
(v) 3 (vi) 7

10. (i) 2 (ii) 9 (iii) 4 (iv) 3
(v) 7 (vi) 5 (vii) 8 (viii) 7
(ix) 6 (x) 2

11. (i) (a) 4 (b) 3 (c) 2 (d) 0
(ii) (a) 3 (b) 0 (c) 1 (d) 2
(iii) (a) 5 (b) 3 (c) 1 (d) 0

Chapter 3 Addition

1. (ii) 7 (iii) 5 (iv) 6 (v) 8 (vi) 6

2. (ii) 6, 2; 8 (iii) 2, 2; 4 (iv) 2, 3; 5
(v) 4, 3; 7 (vi) 3, 2; 5

3. (i) 4, 2; 6 (ii) 4, 5; 9 (iii) 6, 1; 7
(iv) 4, 4; 8 (v) 3, 2; 5 (vi) 4, 6; 10
(vii) 2, 1; 3 (viii) 2, 2; 4

4. (ii)–(a), (iii)–(b), (iv)–(e), (v)–(d)

5. (ii) 3 (iii) 5 (iv) 9 (v) 8

6. (ii)–V–(a), (iii)–I–(e),
(iv)–VI–(d), (v)–II–(b),
(vi)–III–(f)

7. (i) 7 (ii) 8 (iii) 6 (iv) 8
(v) 4 (vi) 9 (vii) 9 (viii) 9
(ix) 8 (x) 5 (xi) 9 (xii) 7

10. (i) 8 (ii) 7 (iii) 8

Chapter 4 Subtraction

1. (ii) 8, 3, 5; 8, 3, 5 (iii) 6, 2, 4; 6, 2, 4
(iv) 6, 3, 3; 6, 3, 3 (v) 9, 2, 7; 9, 2, 7

2. (ii) 8, 2; 6 (iii) 8, 4; 4
(iv) 8, 1; 7 (v) 6, 3; 3

3. (ii) 0 (iii) 1 (iv) 2 (v) 3
(vi) 7 (vii) 9 (viii) 4 (ix) 8
(x) 5

4. (i) 5 (ii) 4 (iii) 2 (iv) 3

5. (i) 4 (ii) 9 (iii) 4 (iv) 8
(v) 0 (vi) 3 (vii) 2 (viii) 5
(ix) 8

7. (i) 5 (ii) 4
(iii) 5 (iv) 3
(v) 3

Chapter **5** Numbers from Ten to Twenty

2. (ii) 13   (iii) 15   (iv) 11   (v) 14   (vi) 17   (vii) 19

3. (ii) 18   (iii) 14   (iv) 17   (v) 20

4. (i) 10 <u>11 12 13</u> Ten <u>Eleven Twelve Thirteen</u>

(ii) 11 <u>12 13 14</u> Eleven <u>Twelve Thirteen Fourteen</u>

(iii) 12 <u>13 14 15</u> Twelve <u>Thirteen Fourteen Fifteen</u>

(iv) 13 <u>14 15 16</u> Thirteen <u>Fourteen Fifteen Sixteen</u>

(v) 14 <u>15 16 17</u> Fourteen <u>Fifteen Sixteen Seventeen</u>

(vi) 15 <u>16 17 18</u> Fifteen <u>Sixteen Seventeen Eighteen</u>

(vii) 16 <u>17 18 19</u> Sixteen <u>Seventeen Eighteen Nineteen</u>

(viii) 17 <u>18 19 20</u> Seventeen <u>Eighteen Nineteen Twenty</u>

5. (i) 13, 15   (ii) 16, 18   (iii) 11, 13   (iv) 14, 16   (v) 17, 19   (vi) 10, 12

6. (i) 16   (ii) 18   (iii) 14   (iv) 17

8. (i) 13   (ii) 14   (iii) 11   (iv) 16   (v) 19   (vi) 19   (vii) 20   (viii) 16

9. (i) 11   (ii) 19   (iii) 14   (iv) 19   (v) 17   (vi) 16   (vii) 18   (viii) 18   (ix) 17   (x) 15

10. (i) 15   (ii) 14   (iii) 13   (iv) 11   (v) 10   (vi) 11

Chapter **6** Time

1. (i) N   (ii) N   (iii) A   (iv) M   (v) M   (vi) E   (vii) A   (viii) M   (ix) E

2. (a) (i) 1   (ii) 3   (iii) 2   (iv) 4

(b) (i) 3   (ii) 2   (iii) 5   (iv) 4   (v) 1

3. (i) (a)   (ii) (b)

Chapter **7** Measurement

1. (i) (a) ✓ (b) ✗   (ii) (a) ✓ (b) ✗   (iii) (a) ✓ (b) ✗   (iv) (a) ✗ (b) ✓   (v) (a) ✗ (b) ✓

2. (i) (a)   (ii) (a)   (iii) (a)   (iv) (c)

3. (i) (b)   (ii) (a)   (iii) (b)   (iv) (a)   (v) (a)

4. (i) (c)   (ii) (c)   (iii) (b)   (iv) (a)

5. (i) (b)   (ii) (a)   (iii) (b)   (iv) (a)

6. (i) (a)   (ii) (b)

7. (i) (a)   (ii) (b)   (iii) (a)   (iv) (b)

8. (i) (a)   (ii) (a)   (iii) (b)   (iv) (c)

Chapter **8** Numbers from Twenty-one to Fifty

1. (ii) 39   (iii) 35   (iv) 48

2. (ii) 30   (iii) 31   (iv) 39   (v) 45   (vi) 48

3. (ii) 43   (iii) 48   (iv) 45   (v) 44   (vi) 48

4. (i) False   (ii) True   (iii) False   (iv) True   (v) False

Chapter **9** **Data Handling**

1. (i) 4 (ii) 3 (iii) 2 (iv) 5
(v) 4 (vi) 3

2. (i) False (ii) True (iii) True

3. (i) (b) 7 (c) 5 (d) 6 (e) 7
(f) 8
(ii) 2 (iii) 1 (iv) 2 (v) 5
(vi) 5 (vii) 2

Chapter **10** **Patterns**

1. (i) P ዋ P (ii) ▢ ▢ △
(iii) ⟵ ⟼ ⟵
(iv) 6 ᘒ 6 (v) ↿ ↾ ↿

Chapter **11** **Numbers**

2. (ii) 63 (iii) 56 (iv) 58 (v) 67

3. (ii) 52 (iii) 54 (iv) 67 (v) 69

4. (ii) 7, 6 (iii) 5, 1 (iv) 8, 2 (v) 9, 6
(vi) 5, 9 (vii) 6, 5 (viii) 8, 4 (ix) 7, 5
(x) 6, 6

5. (i) 78, 79, 81 (ii) 63, 64, 66
(iii) 53, 55, 56, 58 (iv) 20, 22, 24
(v) 71 (vi) 59
(vii) 100

Chapter **12** **Money**

1. (ii)–(f), (iii)–(a), (iv)–(c),
(v)–(b), (vi)–(d)

2. (i) (a) (b) (c)
(d) (e)
(ii) (a) (b)
(c) (d)
(e) (f)
(g)

3. (ii) ₹ 18 (iii) ₹ 16 (iv) ₹ 9

4. (i) ✗ (ii) ✓ (iii) ✗ (iv) ✓
(v) ✓

5. (ii)–(e), (iii)–(a),
(iv)–(b),
(v)–(d)

Chapter **13** **How Many**

1. (i) 7 (ii) 15 (iii) 18 (iv) 33
(v) 68 (vi) 85

2. (i) ₹ 15 (ii) ₹ 8 (iii) ₹ 30 (iv) ₹ 8

3. (i) Sixteen (ii) Twenty three
(iii) Nineteen (iv) Twenty nine
(v) Thirty six
(vi) Thirty one

4. (ii) 4, 6 (iii) 7, 5 (iv) 2, 4
(v) 3, 9 (vi) 6, 2 (vii) 8, 1
(viii) 9, 6 (ix) 4, 3 (x) 5, 1